C# 7 and .NET Core 2.0 High Performance

Build highly performant, multi-threaded, and concurrent applications using C# 7 and .NET Core 2.0

Ovais Mehboob Ahmed Khan

BIRMINGHAM - MUMBAI

C# 7 and .NET Core 2.0 High Performance

Commissioning Editor: Merint Mathew
Acquisition Editor: Chaitanya Nair
Content Development Editor: Anugraha Arunagiri
Technical Editor: Jijo Maliyekal
Copy Editor: Safis Editing
Project Coordinator: Ulhas Kambali
Proofreader: Safis Editing
Indexer: Tejal Daruwale Soni
Graphics: Tania Dutta
Production Coordinator: Deepika Naik

First published: April 2018

Production reference: 1240418

Published by Packt Publishing Ltd.
Livery Place
35 Livery Street
Birmingham
B3 2PB, UK.

ISBN 978-1-78847-004-9

www.packtpub.com

`mapt.io`

Mapt is an online digital library that gives you full access to over 5,000 books and videos, as well as industry leading tools to help you plan your personal development and advance your career. For more information, please visit our website.

Why subscribe?

- Spend less time learning and more time coding with practical eBooks and Videos from over 4,000 industry professionals

- Improve your learning with Skill Plans built especially for you

- Get a free eBook or video every month

- Mapt is fully searchable

- Copy and paste, print, and bookmark content

PacktPub.com

Did you know that Packt offers eBook versions of every book published, with PDF and ePub files available? You can upgrade to the eBook version at `www.PacktPub.com` and as a print book customer, you are entitled to a discount on the eBook copy. Get in touch with us at `service@packtpub.com` for more details.

At `www.PacktPub.com`, you can also read a collection of free technical articles, sign up for a range of free newsletters, and receive exclusive discounts and offers on Packt books and eBooks.

Contributors

About the author

Ovais Mehboob Ahmed Khan is a seasoned programmer and solution architect with over 14 years of software development experience. He has worked in organizations across Pakistan, the USA, and the Middle East. Currently, he is working for a government entity based in Dubai. A Microsoft MVP, he specializes mainly in Microsoft .NET, the cloud and web development. He has published technical articles on MSDN, TechNet, personal blog, and he has authored two other books published by Packt: *JavaScript for .NET Developers* and *Enterprise Application Architecture with .NET Core*.

I would like to thank my family for supporting me, especially my mother, wife, and brother, who have always encouraged me in every goal of my life. My father, may he rest in peace, would have been proud of my achievements.

About the reviewer

Jalpesh Vadgama has been working on technologies like .NET such as MVC, ASP.NET Core, Web Forms, and REST APIs for over 14 years now. Experienced in open source server-side technologies such as Node.js, he has worked with frameworks such as jQuery, Knockout.js, Angular, React.js and Vue. He has been awarded the Microsoft MVP award six times for his technical contribution to .NET and has delivered over 50 Enterprise-level applications using .NET technologies. He has also been using software development methodologies such as Agile, Scrum, and Waterfall for quite a while.

I would like to thank my wife and family for their support.

Packt is searching for authors like you

If you're interested in becoming an author for Packt, please visit `authors.packtpub.com` and apply today. We have worked with thousands of developers and tech professionals, just like you, to help them share their insight with the global tech community. You can make a general application, apply for a specific hot topic that we are recruiting an author for, or submit your own idea.

Table of Contents

Preface

The book begins with an introduction to the new features of C# 7 and .NET Core 2.0, and how they help improve the performance of your application. The book will then help you understand the core internals of .NET Core, which includes the compilation process, garbage collection, utilizing multiple cores of the CPU to develop highly-performant applications, and measuring performance using a powerful library for benchmarking applications named BenchmarkDotNet. We will learn about developing applications and programs using multithreading and asynchronous programming, and how to use those concepts to build efficient applications for faster execution. Next, you'll understand the importance of data structure optimization and how it can be used efficiently. We move on to the patterns and best practices to use when designing applications in .NET Core, along with how to utilize memory in an effective way and avoid memory leakage. After that, we'll talk about implementing security and resiliency in .NET Core applications, and we'll use the Polly framework to implement a circuit breaker, and retry and fallback patterns, along with certain middleware to harden the HTTP pipeline. We'll also implement security such as authorization and authentication using the Identity framework. Moving ahead, we will learn about the microservices architecture and see how we can use it to create applications that are modular, highly scalable, and independently deployable. We end with App Metrics, and will learn how to use it to monitor the performance of your application.

Who this book is for

This book is for .NET developers who want to improve the speed of their application's code or who simply want to take their skills to the next level, where they can develop and produce quality applications that are not only performant but also adhere to the industry best practices. Basic C# knowledge is assumed.

What this book covers

Chapter 1, *What's New in .NET Core 2 and C# 7?*, discusses the .NET Core Framework and covers some improvements that were introduced with .NET Core 2.0. We will also look into the new features of C# 7 and see how we can write cleaner code and simplify syntactic expressions. Lastly, we cover the topic of writing quality code. We'll see how we can leverage the Code analysis feature of Visual Studio 2017 to add analyzers to our project and improve code quality.

Chapter 2, *Understanding .NET Core Internals and Measuring Performance*, discusses the core concepts of .NET Core, including the compilation process, garbage collection, building highly-performant .NET Core applications utilizing multiple cores of the CPU, and publishing an application using a release build. We will also explore the benchmarking tool that is highly used for code optimization and provides results specific to in-memory objects.

Chapter 3, *Multithreading and Asynchronous Programming in .NET Core*, explores the core fundamentals of multithreaded and asynchronous programming. The chapter starts with the basic differences between multithreaded and asynchronous programming and walks you through the core concepts. It explores APIs and how to use them when writing a multithreaded application. We will learn how the Task Programming Library can be used to serve asynchronous operations, and how to implement the Task Asynchronous pattern. Lastly, we will explore parallel programming techniques and some of the best design patterns being used.

Chapter 4, *Data Structures and Writing Optimized Code in C#*, outlines the core concepts of data structures, the types of data structure, and their advantages and disadvantages, followed by the best possible scenarios to which each data structure is suited. We also learn about the Big O notation, which is one of the core topics to consider when writing code and helps developers check the quality of the code and performance. Lastly, we will look into some best practices and cover topics such as boxing and unboxing, string concatenation, exception handling, `for` and `foreach`, and delegates.

Chapter 5, *Designing Guidelines for .NET Core Application Performance*, showcases some coding principles that make application code look clean and easy to understand. If the code is clean, it offers other developers a way to understand it completely and helps in many other ways. We will learn some basic design principles that are considered to be part of the core principles when designing applications. Principles such as KISS, YAGNI, DRY, Separation of Concerns, and SOLID are highly essential in software design, and caching and choosing the right data structure have a significant impact on performance, and can improve performance if they are properly used. Lastly, we will learn some best practices that should be considered when handling communication, resource management, and concurrency.

Chapter 6, *Memory Management Techniques in .NET Core*, outlines the underlying process of how memory management is done in .NET. We will explore the debugging tool, which can be used by developers to investigate the object's memory allocation on the heap. We will also learn about memory fragmentation, finalizers, and how to implement a dispose pattern to clean up resources by implementing the `IDisposable` interface.

Chapter 7, *Securing and Implementing Resilience in .NET Core Applications*, takes you through resiliency, which is a very important factor when developing highly-performant applications in .NET Core. We will learn different policies and use the Polly framework to use those policies in .NET Core. We will also learn about safe storage mechanisms and how to use them in the development environment in order to keep sensitive information separate from the project repository. At the end of this chapter, we will learn some security fundamentals, which include SSL, CSRF, CORS, security headers, and the ASP.NET Core Identity framework, in order to protect ASP.NET Core applications.

Chapter 8, *Microservices Architecture*, looks at the most quickly evolving software architecture for developing highly performant and scalable applications for the cloud based on microservices. We will learn some of the core fundamentals of the microservices architecture, its benefits, and patterns and practices used when designing the architecture. We will discuss certain challenges faced when decomposing enterprise applications into the microservices architecture style and learn patterns such as API composition and CQRS in order to address them. Later in the chapter, we will develop a basic application in .NET Core and discuss the solution's structure and the components of microservices. Then we will develop identity and vendor services.

Chapter 9, *Monitoring Application Performance Using Tools*, dives into key performance metrics that are essential for monitoring an application's performance. We will explore and set up App Metrics, which is a free tool that is cross-platform and provides various extensions that can be used to achieve extensive reporting. We will go through a step-by-step guide on how to configure and set up App Metrics and related components, such as InfluxDb and Grafana, which is used to store and view telemetry in the Grafana web-based tool and integrate it with ASP.NET Core application.

To get the most out of this book

The readers should be equipped with the following configurations of the environment:

1. **Development Environment**: Visual Studio 2015/2017 Community Edition
2. **Execution Environment**: .NET Core
3. **OS Environment**: Windows or Linux

Download the example code files

You can download the example code files for this book from your account at `www.packtpub.com`. If you purchased this book elsewhere, you can visit `www.packtpub.com/support` and register to have the files emailed directly to you.

You can download the code files by following these steps:

1. Log in or register at `www.packtpub.com`.
2. Select the **SUPPORT** tab.
3. Click on **Code Downloads & Errata**.
4. Enter the name of the book in the **Search** box and follow the onscreen instructions.

Once the file is downloaded, please make sure that you unzip or extract the folder using the latest version of:

- WinRAR/7-Zip for Windows
- Zipeg/iZip/UnRarX for Mac
- 7-Zip/PeaZip for Linux

The code bundle for the book is also hosted on GitHub at `https://github.com/PacktPublishing/C-Sharp-7-and-NET-Core-2-High-Performance/`. In case there's an update to the code, it will be updated on the existing GitHub repository.

We also have other code bundles from our rich catalog of books and videos available at `https://github.com/PacktPublishing/`. Check them out!

Download the color images

We also provide a PDF file that has color images of the screenshots/diagrams used in this book. You can download it here: `https://www.packtpub.com/sites/default/files/downloads/CSharp7andNETCore2HighPerformance_ColorImages.pdf`.

Conventions used

There are a number of text conventions used throughout this book.

`CodeInText`: Indicates code words in text, database table names, folder names, filenames, file extensions, pathnames, dummy URLs, user input, and Twitter handles. Here is an example: "Mount the downloaded `WebStorm-10*.dmg` disk image file as another disk on your system."

A block of code is set as follows:

```
public static IWebHost BuildWebHost(string[] args) =>
   WebHost.CreateDefaultBuilder(args)
     .UseMetrics()
     .UseStartup<Startup>()
     .Build();
```

Any command-line input or output is written as follows:

```
Install-Package App.Metrics
Install-Pacakge App.Metrics.AspnetCore.Mvc
```

Bold: Indicates a new term, an important word, or words that you see onscreen. For example, words in menus or dialog boxes appear in the text like this. Here is an example: "Select **System info** from the **Administration** panel."

 Warnings or important notes appear like this.

 Tips and tricks appear like this.

Get in touch

Feedback from our readers is always welcome.

General feedback: Email `feedback@packtpub.com` and mention the book title in the subject of your message. If you have questions about any aspect of this book, please email us at `questions@packtpub.com`.

Errata: Although we have taken every care to ensure the accuracy of our content, mistakes do happen. If you have found a mistake in this book, we would be grateful if you would report this to us. Please visit www.packtpub.com/submit-errata, selecting your book, clicking on the Errata Submission Form link, and entering the details.

Piracy: If you come across any illegal copies of our works in any form on the Internet, we would be grateful if you would provide us with the location address or website name. Please contact us at copyright@packtpub.com with a link to the material.

If you are interested in becoming an author: If there is a topic that you have expertise in and you are interested in either writing or contributing to a book, please visit authors.packtpub.com.

Reviews

Please leave a review. Once you have read and used this book, why not leave a review on the site that you purchased it from? Potential readers can then see and use your unbiased opinion to make purchase decisions, we at Packt can understand what you think about our products, and our authors can see your feedback on their book. Thank you!

For more information about Packt, please visit packtpub.com.

What's New in .NET Core 2 and C# 7? 1

.NET Core is a development platform by Microsoft that runs cross-platform and is maintained by Microsoft and the community at GitHub. It is the most emergent and popular framework in development communities due to its performance and platform portability. It targets every developer that can develop any application for any platform that includes web, cloud, mobile, embedded, and IoT scenarios.

With .NET Core, we can develop applications using C#, F#, and now VB.NET as well. However, C# is the most widely used language among developers.

In this chapter, you will learn the following topics:

- Performance improvements in .NET Core 2.0
- Upgrading the path from .NET Core 1.x to 2.0
- .NET Standard 2.0
- What comes with ASP.NET Core 2.0
- New features in C# 7.0

Evolution of .NET

In early 2002, when Microsoft first introduced the .NET Framework, it targeted developers who were working on classic ASP or VB 6 platforms since they didn't have any compelling framework for developing enterprise-level applications. With the release of the .NET Framework, developers had a platform to develop applications and could choose any of the languages from VB.NET, C#, and F#. Irrespective of the language chosen, the code is interoperable, and developers can create a project with VB.NET and reference it in their C# or F# project and vice versa.

The core component of .NET Framework includes **Common Language Runtime (CLR)**, **Framework Class Libraries (FCL)**, **Base Class Libraries (BCL)**, and a set of application models. New features and patches have been introduced with the newer version of the .NET Framework, which comes with the new release of Windows, and developers have had to wait for a year or so to get those improvements. Every team at Microsoft worked on a different application model, and each team had to wait for the date when the new framework was released to port their fixes and improvements. Windows Forms and Web Forms were the primary application models at that time that were widely used by .NET developers.

When Web Forms was first introduced, it was a breakthrough which attracted both web developers who worked on Classic ASP and desktop application developers who worked on Visual Basic 6.0. The developer experience was appealing and provided a decent set of controls that could easily be dragged and dropped to the screen, followed to their events and properties that could be set either through the view file (`.aspx`) or code-behind files. Later on, Microsoft introduced the **Model View Controller (MVC)** application model that implemented the separation of concerns design principle, so that View, Model, and Controller are separate entities. The View is the user interface that renders the Model, where the Model represents the business entity and holds the data, and the Controller that handles the request and updates the model and injects it into the View. MVC was a breakthrough that let developers write cleaner code and bind their model with the HTML controls using model binding. With the passage of time, more features were added and the core .NET web assembly `System.Web` became quite big and bloated, and contained lots of packages and APIs that were not always useful in every type of application. However, with .NET, several groundbreaking changes were introduced and `System.Web` got split into NuGet packages that can be referenced and added individually based on requirements.

.NET Core (codename .NET vNext) was first introduced in 2014, and the following are the core benefits of using .NET Core:

Benefit	Description
Cross Platform	.NET Core can run on Windows, Linux, and macOS
Host Agnostic	.NET Core on the server side is not dependent on IIS and, with two lightweight servers, *Kestrel* and *WebListener*, it can be self-hosted as a Console application and can be also gelled with mature servers such as IIS, Apache, and others through a reverse proxy option
Modular	Ships as NuGet packages
Open Source	The entire source code is released as open source via the .NET Foundation
CLI tooling	Command line tools to create, build, and run projects from the command line

.NET Core is a cross-platform, open-source framework that implements .NET Standard. It provides a runtime known as .NET Core CLR, framework class libraries, which are primitive libraries known as *CoreFX,* and APIs that are similar to what .NET Framework has, but have a smaller footprint (lesser dependencies on other assemblies):

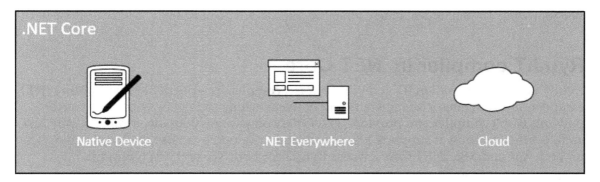

.NET Core provides flexible deployment options as follows:

- **Framework-Dependent Deployment (FDD)**: needs .NET Core SDK to be installed on the machine
- **Self-Contained Deployment (SCD)**: No machine-wide installation of .NET Core SDK is needed on the machine and .NET Core CLR and framework class libraries are part of the application package

To install .NET Core 2.0, you can navigate to the following link `https://www.microsoft.com/net/core` and go through the options for installing it on Windows, Linux, MAC, and Docker.

New improvements in .NET Core 2.0

The most recent version of .NET Core, 2.0, comes with a number of improvements. .NET Core 2.0 is the fastest version of all times and can run on multiple platforms including various Linux distros, macOS (operating system), and Windows.

 Distros stands for Linux distribution (often abbreviated as distro), and it is an operating system made from a software collection, which is based upon the Linux kernel and, often, a package management system.

Performance improvements

.NET Core is more robust and performance efficient and, since it's open source, the Microsoft team with other community members are bringing more improvements.

The following are the improvements that are part of .NET Core 2.0.

RyuJIT compiler in .NET Core

RyuJIT is a next-generation JIT compiler that is a complete rewrite of the **Just In Time** (**JIT**) compiler and generates a lot more efficient native machine code. It is twice as fast as the previous 64-bit compiler and provides 30% faster compilation. Initially, it runs on only X64 architectures, but now it supports X86 as well and developers can use the RyuJIT compiler for both X64 and X86. .NET Core 2.0 uses RyuJIT for both X86 and X64 platforms.

Profile guided optimization

Profile-guided optimization (**PGO**) is a compilation technology used by C++ compiler to generate optimized code. It applies to the internal native compiled components of the runtime and JIT. It performs compilation in two steps, which are as follows:

1. It records the information about code execution.
2. From this information, it generates better code.

The following diagram depicts the life cycle of how the code is compiled:

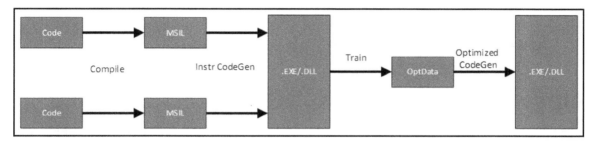

In .NET Core 1.1, Microsoft already released the PGO for Windows X64 architecture, but in .NET Core 2.0, this has been added for both Windows X64 and X86 architectures. Also, as per observatory results, it was noted that the actual startup time is mostly taken by `coreclr.dll` and `clrjit.dll` for Windows. Alternatively, on Linux, there are `libcoreclr.so` and `libclrjit.so`, respectively.

Comparing RyuJIT with the old JIT compiler known as JIT32, RyuJIT is more efficient in code generation. The startup time of the JIT32 was faster than the RyuJIT; however, the code is not efficient. To overcome the initial startup time taken by the RyuJIT compiler, Microsoft used PGO, which brought the performance closer to JIT32 performance and achieved both efficient code and performance on startup.

For Linux, the compiler toolchain is different for each distro, and Microsoft is working on a separate Linux version of .NET that uses the PGO optimizations applicable to all distros.

Simplified packaging

With .NET Core, we can add libraries to our project from NuGet. All framework and third-party libraries can be added as NuGet packages. With a large sized application that refers many libraries, adding each library one by one is a cumbersome process. .NET Core 2.0 has simplified the packaging mechanism and introduced meta-packages that can be added as one single package that contains all the assemblies that are linked to it.

For example, if you wanted to work on ASP.NET Core in .NET Core 2.0, you just have to add one single package, `Microsoft.AspNetCore.All`, using NuGet.

The following is the command that will install this package into your project:

```
Install-Package Microsoft.AspNetCore.All -Version 2.0.0
```

Upgrading path from .NET Core 1.x to 2.0

.NET Core 2.0 comes with lots of improvements, and this is the primary reason people wanted to migrate their existing .NET Core applications from 1.x to 2.0. However, there is a checklist which we will go through in this topic to ensure smooth migration.

1. Install .NET Core 2.0

First of all, install the .NET Core 2.0 SDK on your machine. It will install the latest assemblies to your machine, which will help you to execute further steps.

2. Upgrade TargetFramework

This is the most important step, and this is where the different versions need to be upgraded in the .NET Core project file. Since we know that, with the `.csproj` type, we don't have `project.json`, to modify the framework and other dependencies, we can edit the existing project using any Visual Studio editor and modify the XML.

The XML Node that needs to be changed is the `TargetFramework`. For .NET Core 2.0, we have to change the `TargetFramework` moniker to `netcoreapp2.0`, which is shown as follows:

```
<TargetFramework>netcoreapp2.0</TargetFramework>
```

Next, you can start building the project which will upgrade the .NET Core dependencies to 2.0. However, there is a chance of a few of them still referencing the older version, and upgrading those dependencies needs to be done explicitly using NuGet package manager.

3. Update .NET Core SDK version

If you have `global.json` added to your project, you have to update the SDK version to `2.0.0`, which is shown as follows:

```
{
  "sdk": {
    "version": "2.0.0"
  }
}
```

4. Update .NET Core CLI

.NET Core CLI is also an important section in your .NET Core project file. When migrating, you have to upgrade the version of `DotNetCliToolReference` to `2.0.0`, which is shown as follows:

```
<ItemGroup>
  <DotNetCliToolReference Include=
  "Microsoft.VisualStudio.Web.CodeGeneration.Tools" Version="2.0.0" />
</ItemGroup>
```

There might be more tools added depending on whether you are using Entity Framework Core, User Secrets, and others. You have to update their versions.

Changes in ASP.NET Core Identity

There have been some more improvements and changes to the ASP.NET Core Identity model. Some of the classes are renamed and you can find them at:
`http://docs.microsoft.com/en-us/aspnet/core/migration`.

Exploring .NET Core CLI and New Project Templates

Command Line Interface (**CLI**) is a very popular tool is almost all popular frameworks like Yeoman Generator, Angular, and others. It lends developers access to execute commands to create, build, and run projects, restore packages, and so on.

.NET CLI provides a toolset with a handful commands that can be executed from the command line interface to create .NET Core projects, restore dependencies, and build and run projects. Under the wire, Visual Studio 2015/2017 and Visual Studio Code even uses this tool to perform different options taken by the developers from their IDE; for example, to create a new project using .NET CLI, we can run the following command:

```
dotnet new
```

It will list down the available templates and the short name that can be used while creating the project.

Here is the screenshot containing the list of project templates that can be used to create/scaffold projects using .NET Core CLI:

```
c:\>dotnet new
Usage: new [options]

Options:
  -h, --help          Displays help for this command.
  -l, --list          Lists templates containing the specified name. If no name is specified, lists all templates.
  -n, --name          The name for the output being created. If no name is specified, the name of the current directory is used.
  -o, --output        Location to place the generated output.
  -i, --install       Installs a source or a template pack.
  -u, --uninstall     Uninstalls a source or a template pack.
  --type              Filters templates based on available types. Predefined values are "project", "item" or "other".
  --force             Forces content to be generated even if it would change existing files.
  -lang, --language   Specifies the language of the template to create.


Templates                                    Short Name      Language        Tags
------------------------------------------------------------------------------------------
Console Application                          console         [C#], F#, VB    Common/Console
Class library                                classlib        [C#], F#, VB    Common/Library
Unit Test Project                            mstest          [C#], F#, VB    Test/MSTest
xUnit Test Project                           xunit           [C#], F#, VB    Test/xUnit
ASP.NET Core Empty                           web             [C#], F#        Web/Empty
ASP.NET Core Web App (Model-View-Controller) mvc             [C#], F#        Web/MVC
ASP.NET Core Web App                         razor           [C#]            Web/MVC/Razor Pages
ASP.NET Core with Angular                    angular         [C#]            Web/MVC/SPA
ASP.NET Core with React.js                   react           [C#]            Web/MVC/SPA
ASP.NET Core with React.js and Redux         reactredux      [C#]            Web/MVC/SPA
ASP.NET Core Web API                         webapi          [C#], F#        Web/WebAPI
global.json file                             globaljson                      Config
Nuget Config                                 nugetconfig                     Config
Web Config                                   webconfig                       Config
Solution File                                sln                             Solution
Razor Page                                   page                            Web/ASP.NET
MVC ViewImports                              viewimports                     Web/ASP.NET
MVC ViewStart                                viewstart                       Web/ASP.NET


Examples:
    dotnet new mvc --auth Individual
    dotnet new console
    dotnet new --help
```

And by running the following command, a new ASP.NET Core MVC application will be created:

```
dotnet new mvc
```

The following screenshot shows the provisioning of the new MVC project after running the preceding command. It creates the project in the same directory where the command is running and restores all the dependencies:

```
c:\testproject>dotnet new mvc
The template "ASP.NET Core Web App (Model-View-Controller)" was created successfully.
This template contains technologies from parties other than Microsoft, see https://aka.ms/template-3pn for details.

Processing post-creation actions...
Running 'dotnet restore' on c:\testproject\testproject.csproj...
  Restoring packages for c:\testproject\testproject.csproj...
  Restore completed in 143.61 ms for c:\testproject\testproject.csproj.
  Generating MSBuild file c:\testproject\obj\testproject.csproj.nuget.g.props.
  Generating MSBuild file c:\testproject\obj\testproject.csproj.nuget.g.targets.
  Restore completed in 7.09 sec for c:\testproject\testproject.csproj.

Restore succeeded.
```

To install the .NET Core CLI toolset, there are some native installers available for Windows, Linux, and macOS. These installers can install and set up the .NET CLI tooling on your machine and developers can run the commands from the CLI.

Here is the list of commands with their descriptions that are provided in the .NET Core CLI:

Command	Description	Example
new	Creates a new project based on the template selected	`dotnet new razor`
restore	Restores all the dependencies defined in the project	`dotnet restore`
build	Builds the project	`dotnet build`
run	Runs the source code without any additional compile	`dotnet run`
publish	Packages the application files into a folder for deployment	`dotnet publish`
test	Used to execute unit tests	`dotnet test`

`vstest`	Executes unit tests from specified files	`dotnet vstest [<TEST_FILE_NAMES>]`
`pack`	Packs the code into a NuGet package	`dotnet pack`
`migrate`	Migrates .NET Core preview 2 to .NET Core 1.0	`dotnet migrate`
`clean`	Cleans the output of the project	`dotnet clean`
`sln`	Modifies a .NET Core solution	`dotnet sln`
`help`	Displays the list of commands available to execute through .NET CLI	`dotnet help`
`store`	Stores the specified assemblies in the runtime package store	`dotnet store`

Here are some of the project level commands that can be used to add a new NuGet package, remove an existing one, list references, and others:

Command	Description	Example
`add package`	Adds a package reference to the project	`dotnet add package Newtonsoft.Json`
`remove package`	Removes a package reference from the project	`dotnet remove package Newtonsoft.Json`
`add reference`	Adds a project reference to the project	`dotnet add reference chapter1/proj1.csproj`
`remove reference`	Removes the project reference from the project	`dotnet remove reference chapter1/proj1.csproj`
`list reference`	List down all the project references in the project	`dotnet list reference`

The following are some common Entity Framework Core commands that can be used to add migration, remove migration, update the database, and so on.

Command	Description	Example
`dotnet ef migrations add`	Adds a new migration	`dotnet ef migrations add Initial` - `Initial` is the name of migration
`dotnet ef migrations list`	List available migrations	`dotnet ef migrations list`
`dotnet ef migrations remove`	Remove specific migration	`dotnet ef migrations remove Initial` - `Initial` is the name of migration
`dotnet ef database update`	To update the database to a specified migration	`dotnet ef database update Initial` - `Initial` is the name of migration
`dotnet ef database drop`	Drops the database	`dotnet ef database drop`

Here are some of the server level commands that can be used to delete the NuGet package from its actual source repository from the machine, add NuGet package into its actual source repository on the machine, and so on:

Command	Description	Example
`nuget delete`	Deletes the package from the server	`dotnet nuget delete Microsoft.AspNetCore.App 2.0`
`nuget push`	Pushes a package to the server and publishes it	`dotnet nuget push foo.nupkg`
`nuget locals`	Lists the local NuGet resources	`dotnet nuget locals -l all`
`msbuild`	Builds a project and all of its dependencies	`dotnet msbuild`
`dotnet install script`	The script to install the .NET CLI tools and the shared runtime	`./dotnet-install.ps1 -Channel LTS`

To run the preceding commands, we can use the tool known as dotnet from the command line and specify the actual command followed by that. When the .NET Core CLI is installed, it is set into the PATH variable in Windows OS and can be accessed from any folder. So, for example, if you are at your project root folder and wanted to restore the dependencies, you can just call the following command and it will restore all the dependencies that have been defined in your project file:

```
dotnet restore
```

The preceding command will start restoring the dependencies or project-specific tools, as defined in the project file. The restoration of tools and dependencies are done in parallel:

```
c:\Users\ovais\Source\Repos\Chapter1\Chapter1>dotnet restore
  Restoring packages for c:\Users\ovais\Source\Repos\Chapter1\Chapter1\Chapter1WebApp.csproj...
  Restoring packages for c:\Users\ovais\Source\Repos\Chapter1\Chapter1\Chapter1WebApp.csproj...
  Restore completed in 801.88 ms for c:\Users\ovais\Source\Repos\Chapter1\Chapter1\Chapter1WebApp.csproj.
  Generating MSBuild file c:\Users\ovais\Source\Repos\Chapter1\Chapter1\obj\Chapter1WebApp.csproj.nuget.g.props.
  Restore completed in 1.72 sec for c:\Users\ovais\Source\Repos\Chapter1\Chapter1\Chapter1WebApp.csproj.
```

We can also set the path where packages can be restored by using the `--packages` argument. However, if this is not specified, it uses the `.nuget/packages` folder under the system's user folder. For example, the default NuGet folder for Windows OS is `{systemdrive}:\Users\{user}\.nuget\packages` and `/home/{user}` for Linux OS, respectively.

Understanding .NET Standard

In the .NET ecosystem, there are many runtimes. We have the .NET Framework, which is a full machine-wide framework installed on the Windows operating system and provides app models for **Windows Presentation Foundation** (**WPF**), Windows Forms, and ASP.NET. Then, we have .NET Core, which is targeted at cross-platform operating systems and devices and provides ASP.NET Core, **Universal Windows Platform** (**UWP**), and a Mono runtime that is targeted at Xamarin applications and developers who can use Mono runtime to develop applications on Xamarin and run on iOS, Android, and Windows OS.

The following diagram depicts how the .NET Standard Library provides an abstraction of .NET Framework, .NET Core, and Xamarin with the common building blocks:

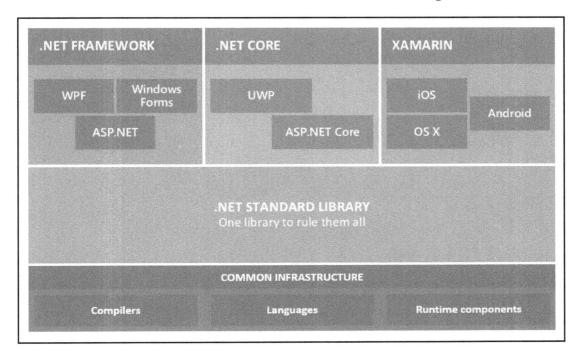

All of these runtimes implement an interface known as .NET Standard, where .NET Standard is the specification of .NET APIs that have the implementation for each runtime. This makes your code portable across different platforms. This means the code created for one runtime can also be executed by another runtime. .NET Standard is the next generation of **Portable Class Libraries (PCL)** we used earlier. Just to recap, PCL is a class library that targets one or more frameworks of .NET. When creating a PCL, we can select the target frameworks where this library needs to be used, and it minimizes the assemblies and uses only those that are common to all frameworks.

The .NET Standard is not an API or executable that can be downloaded or installed. It is a specification that defines the API that each platform implements. Each runtime version implements a specific .NET Standard version. The following table shows the versions of .NET Standard each platform implements:

.NET Standard	.NET Core	.NET Framework (with .NET Core 1.x SDK)	.NET Framework (with .NET Core 2.0 SDK)	Mono	Universal Windows Platform	Windows	Windows Phone	Windows Phone Silverlight	Xamarin.Mac	Xamarin.Android	Xamarin.iOS
1.0		4.5	4.5			8.0		8.0			
1.1							8.1				
1.2		4.5.1	4.5.1		10.0	8.1					
1.3	1.0	4.6	4.6	4.6					3.0	7.0	10.0
1.4		4.6.1									
1.5		4.6.2	4.6.1								
1.6					10.0.16299						
2.0	2.0			5.4					3.8	8.0	10.14

We can see that .NET Core 2.0 implements .NET Standard 2.0 and that .NET Framework 4.5 implements .NET Standard 1.1., so for example, if we have a class library developed on .NET Framework 4.5, this can easily be added into the .NET Core project because it implements a greater version of .NET Standard. On the other hand, if we wanted to reference the .NET Core assembly into .NET Framework 4.5, we can do so by changing the .NET Standard version to 1.1 without recompiling and building our project.

As we learned, the basic idea of .NET Standard is to share code between different runtimes, but how it differs from PCL is shown as follows:

Portable Class Library (PCL)	.NET Standard
Represents the Microsoft platform and targets a limited set of platforms	Agnostic to platform
APIs are defined by the platforms you target	Curated set of APIs
They are not linearly versioned	Linearly versioned

.NET Standard is also mapped to PCL, so if you have an existing PCL library that you wanted to convert to .NET Standard, you can reference the following table:

PCL Profile	.NET Standard	PCL Plaforms
7	1.1	.NET Framework 4.5, Windows 8
31	1.0	Windows 8.1, Windows Phone Silverlight 8.1
32	1.2	Windows 8.1, Windows Phone 8.1
44	1.2	.NET Framework 4.5.1, Windows 8.1
49	1.0	.NET Framework 4.5, Windows Phone Silverlight 8
78	1.0	.NET Framework 4.5, Windows 8, Windows Phone Silverlight 8
84	1.0	Windows Phone 8.1, Windows Phone Silverlight 8.1
111	1.1	.NET Framework 4.5, Windows 8, Windows Phone 8.1
151	1.2	.NET Framework 4.5.1, Windows 8.1, Windows Phone 8.1
157	1.0	Windows 8.1, Windows Phone 8.1, Windows Phone Silverlight 8.1

259	1.0	.NET Framework 4.5, Windows 8, Windows Phone 8.1, Windows Phone Silverlight 8

Considering the preceding table, if we have a PCL that targets .NET Framework 4.5.1, Windows 8.1, and Windows Phone 8.1 with the PCL profile set to 151, it can be converted to the .NET Standard library with version 1.2.

Versioning of .NET Standard

Unlike PCL, each version of .NET Standard is linearly versioned and contains the APIs for the previous versions and so on. Once the version is shipped, it is frozen and cannot be changed, and the application can easily target that version.

The following diagram is a representation of how .NET Standard is versioned. The higher the version is, the more APIs will be available, whereas the lower the version is, the more platforms will be available:

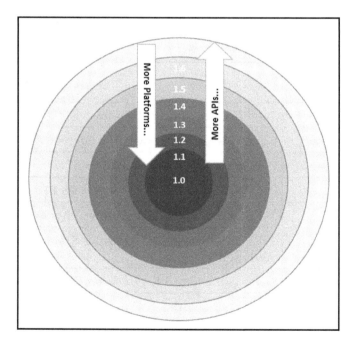

New improvements in .NET Standard 2.0

.NET Core 2.0 is targeted at .NET Standard 2.0 and provides two major benefits. This includes the increase in the number of APIs provided from the previous version and its compatibility mode, as we will discuss further in this chapter.

More APIs in .NET Standard 2.0

More APIs have been added into .NET Standard 2.0 and the number is almost double that of the previous .NET Standard, 1.0. Additionally APIs like DataSet, collections, binary serialization, XML schema, and others are now part of .NET Standard 2.0 specification. This has increased the portability of code from .NET Framework to .NET Core.

The following diagram depicts the categorical view of APIs added in each area:

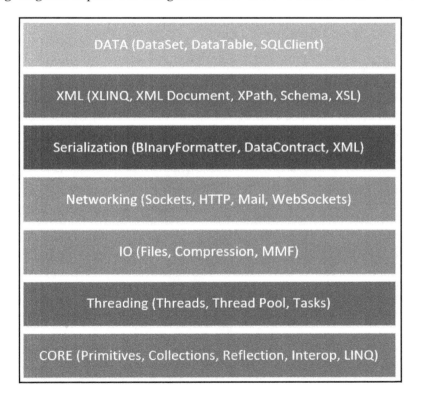

Compatibility mode

Although more than 33K APIs have been added into .NET Standard 2.0, many of the NuGet packages still target .NET Framework, and moving them to .NET Standard is not possible, since their dependencies are still not targeted at .NET Standard. However, with .NET Standard 2.0, we can still add packages which show a warning but don't block adding those packages into our .NET Standard library.

Under the hood, .NET Standard 2.0 uses compatibility shim, which solves the third party library compatibility issue and makes it easy in referencing those libraries. In the CLR world, the identity of the assembly is part of the type identity. This means that when we say `System.Object` in .NET Framework, we are referencing `[mscorlib]System.Object` and with .NET Standard, we are referencing `[netstandard]System.Object`, so if we are referencing any assembly which is part of .NET Framework, it cannot be easily run on .NET Standard and so compatibility issues arise. To solve this problem, they have used type forwarding which provides a fake `mscorlib` assembly that type forwards all the types to the .NET Standard implementation.

Here is a representation of how the .NET Framework libraries can run in any of the .NET Standard implementations using the type forwarding approach:

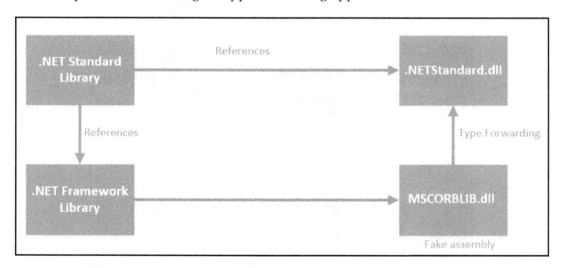

On the other hand, if we have a .NET Framework library and we wanted to reference a .NET Standard library, it will add the `netstandard` fake assembly and perform type forwarding of all the types by using the .NET Framework implementation:

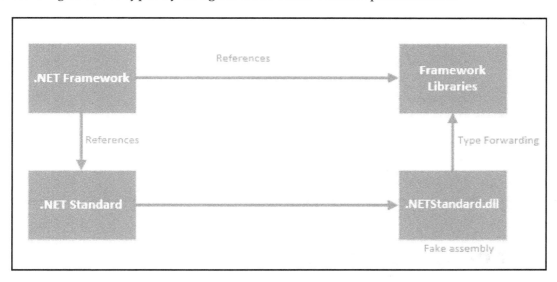

 To suppress warnings, we can add NU1701 for particular NuGet packages whose dependencies are not targeting .NET Standard.

Creating a .NET Standard library

To create a .NET Standard library, you can either use Visual Studio or the .NET Core CLI toolset. From Visual Studio, we can just click on the .NET Standard option as shown in the following screenshot, and select **Class Library** (.NET Standard).

Once the .NET Standard library is created, we can reference it to any project and change the version if needed, depending on which platform we want to reference. The version can be changed from the properties panel, as shown in the following screenshot:

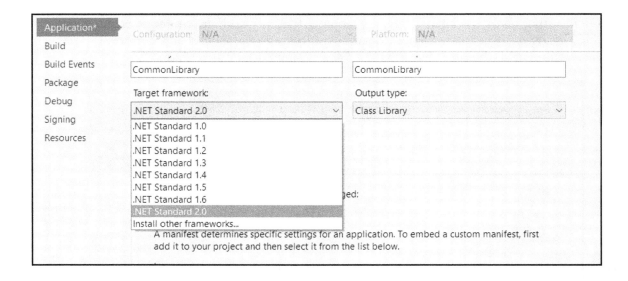

What comes with ASP.NET Core 2.0

ASP.NET Core is one of the most powerful platforms for developing cloud-ready and enterprise web applications that run cross-platform. Microsoft has added many features with ASP.NET Core 2.0, and that includes new project templates, Razor Pages, simplified provisioning of Application Insights, connection pooling, and so on.

The following are some new improvements for ASP.NET Core 2.0.

ASP.NET Core Razor Pages

Razor syntax-based pages have been introduced in ASP.NET Core. Now, developers can develop applications and write syntax on the HTML with no controller in place. Instead, there is a code behind file where other events and logic can be handled. The backend page class is inherited from the `PageModel` class and its member variables and methods can be accessed using the `Model` object in Razor syntax. The following is a simple example that contains the `GetTitle` method defined in the `code-behind` class and used in the view page:

```
public class IndexModel : PageModel
{
  public string GetTitle() => "Home Page";
}
```

Here is the `Index.cshtml` file that displays the date by calling the `GetCurrentDate` method:

```
@page
@model IndexModel
@{
  ViewData["Title"] = Model.GetTitle();
}
```

Automatic Page and View compilation on publishing

On publishing the ASP.NET Core Razor pages project, all the views are compiled into one single assembly and the published folder size is comparatively small. In case we want view and all the `.cshtml` files to be generated when the publishing process takes place, we have to add an entry, which is shown as follows:

```
<Project Sdk="Microsoft.NET.Sdk.Web">
  <PropertyGroup>
    <TargetFramework>netcoreapp2.0</TargetFramework>
    <MvcRazorCompileOnPublish>false</MvcRazorCompileOnPublish>
  </PropertyGroup>
```

Razor support for C# 7.1

Now, we can use C# 7.1 features such as inferred tuple names, pattern matching with generics, and expressions. In order to add this support, we have to add one XML tag as follows in our project file:

```
<LangVersion>latest</LangVersion>
```

Simplified configuration for Application Insights

With ASP.NET Core 2.0, you can enable Application Insights with a single click. A user can enable Application Insights by just right clicking **Project** and hitting **Add | Application Insights Telemetry** before going through a simple wizard. This allows you to monitor the application and provides complete diagnostics information from Azure Application Insights.

We can also view the complete telemetry from the Visual Studio 2017 IDE from the Application Insights Search window and monitor trends from Application Insights Trends. Both of these windows can be opened from the **View | Other Windows menu**.

Pooling connections in Entity Framework Core 2.0

With the recent release of Entity Framework Core 2.0, we can pool connections by using the `AddDbContextPool` method in the `Startup` class. As we already know, in ASP.NET Core, we have to add the `DbContext` object using **Dependency Injection (DI)** in the `ConfigureServices` method in the `Startup` class, and when it is used in the controller, a new instance of the `DbContext` object is injected. To optimize performance, Microsoft has provided this `AddDbContextPool` method, which first checks for the available database context instance and injects it wherever it is needed. On the other hand, if the database context instance is not available, a new instance is created and injected.

The following code shows how `AddDbContext` can be added in the `ConfigureServices` method in the `Startup` class:

```
services.AddDbContextPool<SampleDbContext>(
  options => options.UseSqlServer(connectionString));
```

 There are some more features added to **Owned Types**, **Table splitting**, **Database Scalar Function** mapping, and string interpolation that you can refer to from the following link:
https://docs.microsoft.com/en-us/ef/core/what-is-new/.

New features in C# 7.0

C# is the most popular language in the .NET ecosystem and was first introduced with the .NET Framework in 2002. The current stable version of C# is 7. The following chart shows how C# 7.0 has progressed and what versions were introduced in different years:

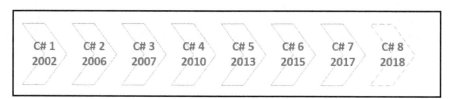

Here are some of the new features that were introduced with C# 7.0:

- Tuples
- Pattern matching
- Reference returns
- Exceptions as expressions
- Local functions
- Out variables Literals
- Async Main

Tuples

Tuples solve the problem of returning more than one value from a method. Traditionally, we can use out variables that are reference variables, and the value is changed if they are modified from the calling method. However, without parameters, there are some limitations, such as that it cannot be used with `async` methods and is not recommended to be used with external services.

Tuples have the following characteristics:

- They are value types.
- They can be converted to other Tuples.
- Tuple elements are public and mutable.

A Tuple is represented as `System.Tuple<T>`, where `T` could be any type. The following example shows how a Tuple can be used with the method and how the values can be invoked:

```
static void Main(string[] args)
{
  var person = GetPerson();
  Console.WriteLine($"ID : {person.Item1},
  Name : {person.Item2}, DOB : {person.Item3}");
}
static (int, string, DateTime) GetPerson()
{
  return (1, "Mark Thompson", new DateTime(1970, 8, 11));
}
```

As you may have noticed, items are dynamically named and the first item is named Item1, the second Item2, and so on. On the other hand, we can also name the items so that the calling party should know about the value, and this can be done by adding the parameter name for each parameter in the Tuple, which is shown as follows:

```
static void Main(string[] args)
{
  var person = GetPerson();
  Console.WriteLine($"ID : {person.id}, Name : {person.name},
  DOB : {person.dob}");
}
static (int id, string name, DateTime dob) GetPerson()
{
  return (1, "Mark Thompson", new DateTime(1970, 8, 11));
}
```

 To learn more about Tuples, please check the following link: https://docs.microsoft.com/en-us/dotnet/csharp/tuples.

Patterns

Patterns matching is the process of performing syntactical testing of the value to verify whether it matches the certain model. There are three types of patterns:

- Constant patterns.
- Type patterns.
- Var patterns.

Constant pattern

A constant pattern is a simple pattern that checks for the constant value. Consider the following example: if the Person object is null, it will return and exit the body method.

The Person class is as follows:

```
class Person
{
  public int ID { set; get; }
  public string Name { get; set; }
```

```
public DateTime DOB { get; set; }
}
```

In the preceding code snippet, we have a `Person` class that contains three properties, namely `ID`, `Name`, and `DOB` (Date of Birth).

The following statement checks for the `person` object with a null constant value and returns it if the object is null:

```
if (person is null) return;
```

Type pattern

The type pattern can be used with an object to verify whether it matches the type or suffices the expression based on the conditions specified. Suppose we need to check whether the `PersonID` is int; assign that `ID` to another variable, `i`, and use it in the program, otherwise return:

```
if (!(person.ID is int i)) return;

Console.WriteLine($"Person ID is {i}");
```

We can also use multiple logical operators to evaluate more conditions, as follows:

```
if (!(person.ID is int i) && !(person.DOB>DateTime.Now.AddYears(-20)))
return;
```

The preceding statement checks whether the `Person.ID` is null or not and whether the person is older than 20.

Var pattern

The var pattern checks if the `var` is equal to some type. The following example shows how the `var` pattern can be used to check for the type and print the `Type` name:

```
if (person is var Person) Console.WriteLine($"It is a person object and
type is {person.GetType()}");
```

 To learn more about patterns, you can refer to the following link: `https://docs.microsoft.com/en-us/dotnet/csharp/whats-new/csharp-7#pattern-matching`.

Reference returns

Reference returns allows a method to return an object as a reference instead of its value. We can define the reference return value by adding a `ref` keyword before the type in the method signature and when returning the object from the method itself.

Here is the signature of the method that allows reference returns:

```
public ref Person GetPersonInformation(int ID);

Following is the implementation of the GetPersonInformation method that
uses the ref keyword while returning the person's object.

Person _person;
public ref Person GetPersonInformation(int ID)
{
  _person = CallPersonHttpService();
  return ref _person;
}
```

Expression bodied member extended

Expression bodied members were introduced in C# 6.0 where the syntactical expression of the method can be written in a simpler way. In C# 7.0, we can use this feature with a constructor, a destructor, an exception, and so on.

The following example shows how the constructor and destructor syntactic expressions can be simplified using expression bodied members:

```
public class PersonManager
{
  //Member Variable
  Person _person;

  //Constructor
  PersonManager(Person person) => _person = person;

  //Destructor
  ~PersonManager() => _person = null;
}
```

With properties, we can also simplify the syntactic expression, and the following is a basic example of how this can be written:

```
private String _name;
```

```
public String Name
{
  get => _name;
  set => _name = value;
}
```

We can also use an expression bodied syntactic expression with exceptions and simplify the expression, which is shown as follows:

```
private String _name;
public String Name
{
  get => _name;
  set => _name = value ?? throw new ArgumentNullException();
}
```

In the preceding example, if the value is null, a new `ArgumentNullException` will be thrown.

Creating Local Functions

Functions that are created within a function are known as Local Functions. These are mainly used when defining helper functions that have to be in the scope of the function itself. The following example shows how the factorial of the number can be obtained by writing a Local Function and calling it recursively:

```
static void Main(string[] args)
{
  Console.WriteLine(ExecuteFactorial(4));
}

static long ExecuteFactorial(int n)
{
  if (n < 0) throw new ArgumentException("Must be non negative",
  nameof(n));
  else return CheckFactorial(n);

  long CheckFactorial(int x)
  {
    if (x == 0) return 1;
    return x * CheckFactorial(x - 1);
  }
}
```

Out variables

With C# 7.0, we can write cleaner code when using out variables. As we know, to use out variables, we have to first declare them. With the new language enhancement, we can now just write out as a prefix and specify the name of the variable that we need that value to be assigned to.

To clarify this concept, we will first see the traditional approach, which is shown as follows:

```
public void GetPerson()
{
  int year;
  int month;
  int day;
  GetPersonDOB(out year, out month, out day);
}

public void GetPersonDOB(out int year, out int month, out int day )
{
  year = 1980;
  month = 11;
  day = 3;
}
```

And here with C# 7.0, we can simplify the preceding GetPerson method, which is shown as follows:

```
public void GetPerson()
{
  GetPersonDOB(out int year, out int month, out int day);
}
```

Async Main

As we already know, in .NET Framework, the Main method is the main entry point from where the application/program is executed by the OS. For example, in ASP.NET Core, Program.cs is the main class where the Main method is defined, which creates a WebHost object, runs the Kestrel server, and loads up the HTTP pipeline as configured in the Startup class.

In the previous version of C#, the `Main` method had the following signatures:

```
public static void Main();
public static void Main(string[] args);
public static int Main();
public static int Main(string[] args);
```

In C# 7.0, we can use Async Main to perform asynchronous operations. The Async/Await feature was initially released in .NET Framework 4.5 in order to execute methods asynchronously. Today, many APIs provides Async/Await methods to perform asynchronous operations.

Here are some additional signatures of the `Main` method that have been added with C# 7.1:

```
public static Task Main();
public static Task Main(string[] args);
public static Task<int> Main();
public static Task<int> Main(string[] args);
```

Because of the preceding async signatures, we can now call `async` methods from the `Main` entry point itself and use await to perform an asynchronous operation. Here is a simple example of ASP.NET Core that calls the `RunAsync` method instead of `Run`:

```
public class Program
{
  public static async Task Main(string[] args)
  {
    await BuildWebHost(args).RunAsync();
  }
  public static IWebHost BuildWebHost(string[] args) =>
    WebHost.CreateDefaultBuilder(args)
    .UseStartup<Startup>()
    .Build();
}
```

Async Main is a feature of C# 7.1, and to enable this feature in Visual Studio 2017, you can go to the project properties, click on the **Advance** button and set the **Language version** as **C# latest minor version (latest)**, which is shown as follows:

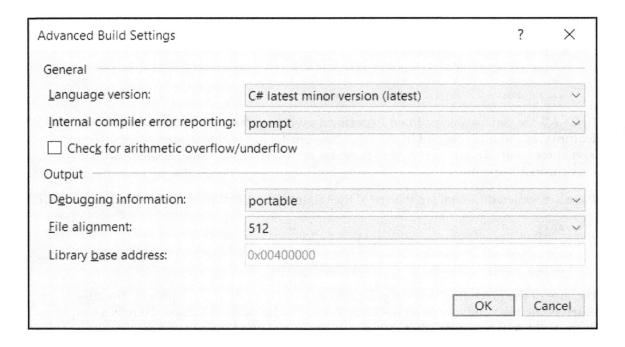

Writing quality code

For every performance-efficient application, code quality plays an important role. As we already know, Visual Studio is the most popular **Integrated Development Environment (IDE)** for developing .NET applications, and since Roslyn (.NET Compiler SDK) exposes compiler platforms as APIs, many features have been introduced that do not only extend the capabilities of Visual Studio, but enhance the development experience.

Live Static Code analysis is one of the core features that can be used in Visual Studio in developing .NET applications which provides code analysis during development while writing code. As this feature uses the Roslyn APIs, many other third-party companies have also introduced sets of analyzers that can be used. We can also develop our own analyzer for a particular requirement, and it's not a very complicated procedure. Let's look at a quick introduction on how we can use Live Static Code analysis in our .NET Core project and how it benefits the development experience by analyzing code and giving warnings, errors, and potential fixes for them.

We can add analyzer as a NuGet package. In NuGet.org, there are many analyzers available, and once we add any analyzer into our project, it adds a new *Analyzer* node into the *Dependencies* section of the project. We can then customize rules, suppress warnings or errors, and so on.

Let's add a new analyzer from Visual Studio in our .NET Core project. If you don't know which analyzer you want to add, you can just type *analyzers* in the NuGet Package manager window and it will list all the analyzers for you. We will just add the `Microsoft.CodeQuality.Analyzers` analyzer, which contains some decent rules:

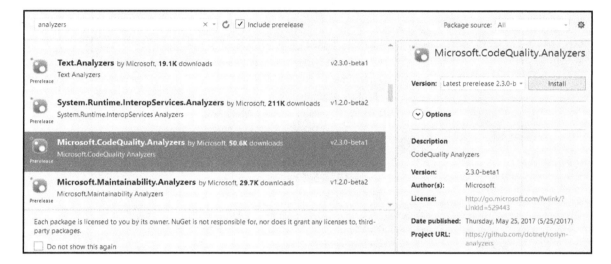

Once the selected Analyzer is added, a new `Analyzers` node is added into our project:

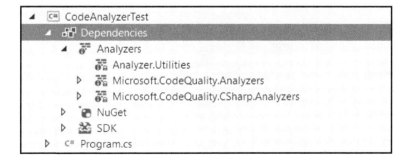

In the preceding picture, we can see that three nodes have been added to the `Analyzers` node, and to see/manage the rules, we can expand the subnodes `Microsoft.CodeQuality.Analyzers` and `Microsoft.CodeQuality.CSharp.Analyzers`, which is shown as follows:

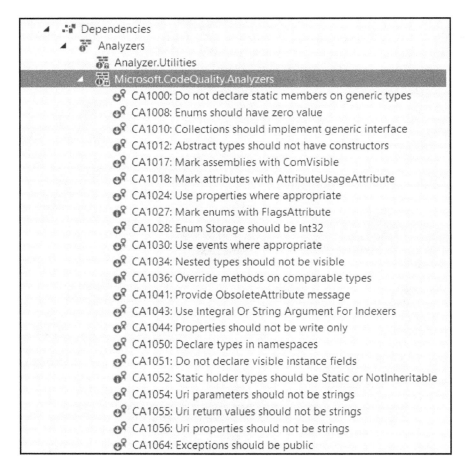

Moreover, we can also change the rule severity by right-clicking on the rule and selecting the severity, which is shown as follows:

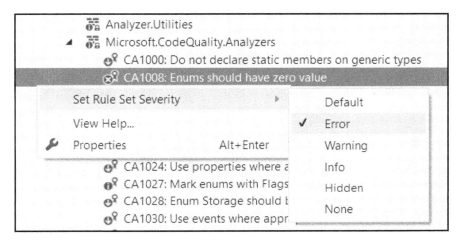

In the preceding picture, rule **CA1008** states that Enums should have a value of zero. Let's test this out and see how it works.

Create a simple `Enum` and specify the values, which are shown as follows:

```
public enum Status
{
   Create =1,
   Update =2,
   Delete =3,
}
```

You will notice as soon as you write this code, it will show the following error and it will provide potential fixes:

```
public enum Status
{
    Create =1,
    Update =2,
    Delete =3,
}
}
```

enum CodeAnalyzerTest.Program.Status

Add a member to Status that has a value of zero with a suggested name of 'None'.

Show potential fixes (Alt+Enter or Ctrl+.)

Finally, here is the fix we can apply, and the error will disappear:

```
0 references
public enum Status
{
    Create =
    Update =     Add a zero-valued member 'None' to enum.    ▶    ⊙ ✖ CA1008 Add a member to Status that has a value of zero with
    Delete =3,                                                      suggested name of 'None'.
}                                                              ...
                                                              {
                                                                  None,
                                                                  Create =1,
                                                              ...

                                                              Preview changes
```

You can also use one of the popular Visual Studio extensions known as Roslynator, which can be downloaded from the following link. It contains more than 190 analyzers and refactorings for C# based projects: `https://marketplace.visualstudio.com/items?itemName=josefpihrt.Roslynator`.

Live Static Code analysis is a great feature that helps developers to write quality code that conforms to the best guidelines and practices.

Summary

In this chapter, we learned about the .NET Core Framework and some new improvements that are introduced with .NET Core 2.0. We also looked into the new features of C# 7 and how we can write cleaner code and simplify syntactic expressions. Finally, we covered the topic of writing quality code and how we can leverage with the Code analysis feature provided in Visual Studio 2017 to add analyzers into our project which serve our needs. The next chapter will be an in-depth chapter about .NET Core that will cover topics around .NET Core internals and performance improvements.

2
Understanding .NET Core Internals and Measuring Performance

When developing application architecture, knowing the internals of how the .NET framework works plays a vital role in ensuring the quality of the application's performance. In this chapter, we will focus on the internals of .NET Core that can help us write quality code and architecture for any application. This chapter will cover some of the core concepts of .NET Core internals, including the compilation process, garbage collection, and **Framework Class Library** (**FCL**). We will complete this chapter by going through the *BenchmarkDotNet* tool, which is mostly used in measuring code performance, and is highly recommended for benchmarking code snippets within an application.

In this chapter, you will learn the following topics:

- .NET Core internals
- Utilizing multiple cores of the CPU for high performance
- How releasing builds increases performance
- Benchmarking .NET Core 2.0 applications

.NET Core internals

.NET Core contains two core components—the runtime CoreCLR and the base-class libraries CoreFX. In this section, we will cover the following topics:

- CoreFX
- CoreCLR
- Understanding MSIL, CLI, CTS, and CLS

- How CLR works
- From compilation to execution—under the hood
- Garbage collection
- .NET Native and JIT compilation

CoreFX

CoreFX is the code name of .NET Core's set of libraries. It contains all the libraries that start with Microsoft.* or System.*and contains collections, I/O, string manipulation, reflection, security, and many more features.

The CoreFX is runtime agnostic, and it can run on any platform regardless of what APIs it supports.

 To learn more about each assembly, you can refer to the .NET Core source browser at `https://source.dot.net`.

CoreCLR

CoreCLR provides the common language runtime environment for .NET Core applications, and manages the execution of the complete application life cycle. It performs various operations when the program is running. Operations such as memory allocation, garbage collection, exception handling, type safety, thread management, and security are part of CoreCLR.

.NET Core's runtime provides the same **Garbage Collection** (**GC**) as .NET Framework and a new **Just In Time** (**JIT**) compiler that is more optimized, codenamed *RyuJIT*. When .NET Core was first released, it was only supported for 64-bit platforms, but with the release of .NET Core 2.0, it is now available for 32-bit platforms as well. However, the 32-bit version is only supported by Windows operating systems.

Understanding MSIL, CLI, CTS, and CLS

When we build our project, the code is compiled into the **Intermediate Language** (**IL**), also known as **Microsoft Intermediate Language** (**MSIL**). MSIL is compliant with the **Common Language Infrastructure** (**CLI**), where CLI is the standard that provides a common type system and a language specification, respectively known as the **Common Type System** (**CTS**) and **Common Language Specification** (**CLS**).

The CTS provides a common type system and compiles the language-specific types into the compliant data types. It standardizes all the .NET languages' data types to a common data type for language interoperability. For example, if the code is written in C#, it will be converted to the specific CTS.

Suppose we have two variables, defined in the following code fragment using C#:

```
class Program
{
  static void Main(string[] args)
  {
    int minNo = 1;
    long maxThroughput = 99999;
  }
}
```

On compilation, the compiler generates the MSIL into an assembly that will be available through the CoreCLR to perform the JIT and convert it into the native machine code. Note that the int and long types are converted to the int32 and int64 respectively:

```
.method private hidebysig static void  Main(string[] args) cil managed
{
  .entrypoint
  // Code size       11 (0xb)
  .maxstack  1
  .locals init (int32 V_0,
           int64 V_1)
  IL_0000:  nop
  IL_0001:  ldc.i4.1
  IL_0002:  stloc.0
  IL_0003:  ldc.i4     0x1869f
  IL_0008:  conv.i8
  IL_0009:  stloc.1
  IL_000a:  ret
} // end of method Program::Main
```

It is not necessary for every language to comply completely with the CTS, and it can support the smaller footprint of the CTS, too. For example, when VB.NET was first released in .NET Framework, it only supported the signed integer data types, and there was no provision to use unsigned integers. With later versions of .NET Framework, and now with .NET Core 2.0, we can use all managed languages, such as C#, F#, and VB.NET, to develop applications and easily reference any project's assembly.

How the CLR works

The CLR is implemented as a set of in-process libraries that are loaded with the application, and runs inside the context of the application process. In the following diagram, we have two .NET Core applications running, named **App1.exe** and **App2.exe**. Each black box represents the application process address space, where the applications **App1.exe** and **App2.exe** are running their own CLR version side by side:

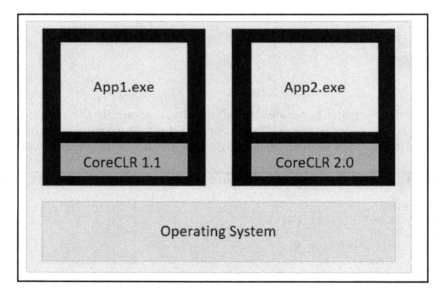

When packaging the .NET Core applications, we can either publish them as **framework-dependent deployments (FDDs)** or **self-contained deployments (SCDs)**. In FDDs, the published package does not contain the .NET Core runtime, and expects that the .NET Core is present on the target/hosting system. With SCDs, all the components, such as the .NET Core runtime and .NET Core libraries, are included in the published package, and the .NET Core installation on the target system is not required.

> To learn more about FDDs or SCDs, please refer to `https://docs.microsoft.com/en-us/dotnet/core/deploying/`.

From compilation to execution – Under the hood

The .NET Core compilation process is like the one used with the .NET Framework. When the project is built, the internal .NET CLI command is invoked by the MSBuild system, which builds the project and generates the assembly (`.dll`) or executable (`.exe`) file. This assembly contains the manifest that contains the assembly's metadata, and includes the version number, culture, type-reference information, information about the referenced assemblies, and a list of other files in the assembly and their association. This assembly manifest is stored either in the MSIL code or in a standalone **portable executable (PE)** file:

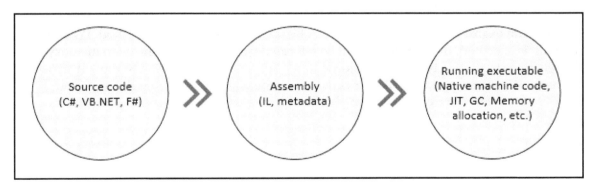

Now, when the executable is run, a new process is started and bootstraps the .NET Core runtime, which then initializes the execution environment, sets up the heap and thread pool, and loads the assembly into the process address space. Based on the program, it then executes the main entry point method (`Main`) and performs a JIT compilation. From here, the code starts executing and the objects start allocating memory on heap, where primitive types store on stack. For each method, the JIT compilation is done and the native machine code gets generated.

When JIT compilation is done, and before generating a native machine code, however, it also performs a few validations. These validations include the following:

- Verifying, that the MSIL was generated during the build process
- Verifying, whether any code was modified or new types added during the JIT compilation process
- Verifying, that the optimized code for the target machine has been generated

Garbage collection

One of the most important features of CLR is the garbage collector. Since the .NET Core applications are managed applications, most of the garbage collection is done automatically by the CLR. The allocation of objects in the memory is efficiently done by the CLR. The CLR not only tunes the virtual memory resources from time to time, but it also reduces the fragmentation of underlying virtual memory to make it more efficient in terms of space.

When the program is run, the objects start allocating memory on the heap and each object's address is stored on the stack. This process continues until the memory reaches its maximum limit. Then the GC comes into play and starts reclaiming memory by removing the unused managed objects and allocating new objects. This is all done automatically by the GC, but there is also a way to invoke the GC to perform garbage collection by calling the `GC.Collect` method

Let's take an example where we have a `Car` object called `c` in the `Main` method. When the function is executed, the `Car` object will be allocated by the CLR into the heap memory and the reference to that `c` object will be stored in the stack address pointing to the `Car` object on the heap. When the garbage collector runs, it reclaims the memory from the heap and removes the reference from the stack:

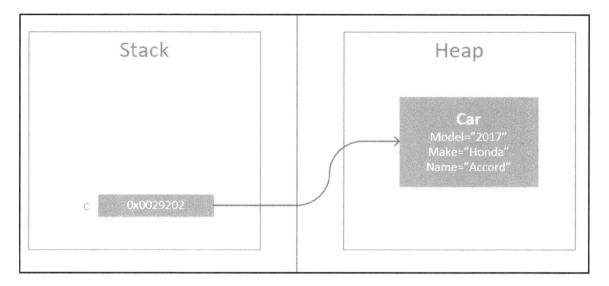

Some important points to note are that the garbage collection is done automatically by the GC on managed objects, and that if there are any unmanaged objects, such as database connections, I/O operations, and so on, they need to be garbage collected explicitly. Otherwise, GC works efficiently on managed objects and ensures that the application will not experience any decrease in performance when the GC is performed.

Generations in GC

There are three kinds of generation in garbage collection known as **Generation 0**, **Generation 1**, and **Generation 2**. In this section, we will look at the concept of generations and how it affects the performance of the garbage collector.

Let's suppose we run an application that creates three objects named **Object1**, **Object2**, and **Object3**. These objects will allocate the memory in **Generation 0**:

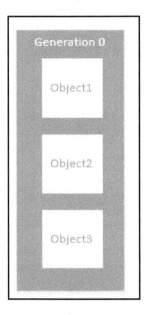

Now, when the garbage collector runs (this is an automatic process, unless you explicitly call the garbage collector from the code), it checks for the objects that are not needed by the application and have no reference in the program. It will simply remove those objects. For example, if the scope of **Object1** is not referenced anywhere, the memory for this object will be reclaimed. However, the other two objects, **Object1** and **Object2**, are still referenced in the program, and will be moved to **Generation 1**.

Now, let's suppose two more objects, called **Object4** and **Object5,** are created. We will store them in the **Generation 0** slot, as shown in the following diagram:

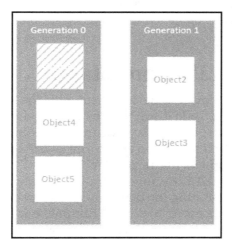

When garbage collection runs the second time, it will find two objects called **Object4** and **Object5** in **Generation 0** and two objects called **Object2** and **Object3** in **Generation 1**. Garbage collector will first check the reference of those objects in **Generation 0** and, if they are not used by the application, they will be removed. The same goes for the **Generation 1** objects. For example, if **Object3** is still referenced, it will be moved to **Generation 2** and **Object2** will be removed from **Generation 1**, as shown in the following diagram:

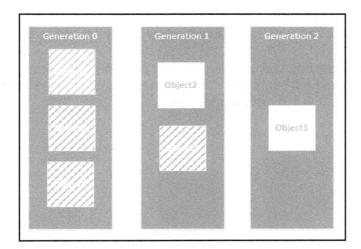

This concept of generations actually optimizes the performance of GC, and the objects stored in **Generation 2** are more likely to be stored for a longer period. GC performs fewer visits and gains time instead of checking each object again and again. The same goes for **Generation 1**, which is also less likely to reclaim the space than **Generation 0**.

.NET Native and JIT compilation

JIT compilation is done mostly at runtime, and it converts the MSIL code to the native machine code. This is when the code is run the first time, and it takes a little bit more time than its successive runs. In .NET Core today, we are developing applications for mobile and handheld devices that have limited resources in terms of CPU power and memory. Currently, the **Universal Windows Platform** (**UWP**) and the Xamarin platform run on .NET Core. With these platforms, .NET Core automatically generates that native assembly at compilation time or while generating the platform-specific packages. Though it does not require the JIT compilation process to be done at runtime, this eventually increases the performance of the application's boot-up time. This native compilation is done through a component known as .NET Native.

.NET Native begins the compilation process after the language-specific compiler finishes up the compilation process that is done at build time. The .NET Native toolchain reads the MSIL generated from the language compiler and performs the following operations:

- It eliminates the metadata from the MSIL.
- It replaces the code that relies on reflection and metadata with the static native code when comparing field values.
- It checks the code that is invoked by the application and includes only that in the final assembly.
- It replaces the full CLR with a refactored runtime that contains the garbage collector and no JIT compiler. The refactored runtime goes with the app and is contained in the assembly named `mrt100_app.dll`.

Utilizing multiple cores of the CPU for high performance

These days, the nature of applications focuses more on connectivity, and there are cases where their operations take more time to execute. We also know that nowadays, all computers come with a multi-core processor, and using these cores effectively increases the performance of the application. Operations such as network/IO have latency issues, and the synchronous execution of the application program may often lead to a long waiting time. If the long-running tasks are executed in a separate thread or in an asynchronous manner, the resulting operation will take less time and increase responsiveness. Another benefit is performance that actually utilizes multiple cores of the processor and executes the task simultaneously. In the .NET world, we can achieve responsiveness and performance by splitting the tasks into multiple threads and using classic multithreading programming APIs, or a more simplified and advanced model known as the **task programming library** (**TPL**). The TPL is now supported in .NET Core 2.0, and we will soon explore how it can be used to execute tasks on multiple cores.

The TPL programming model is based on the task. A task is a unit of work—an object's representation of an ongoing operation.

A simple task can be created by writing the following lines of code:

```
static void Main(string[] args)
{
  Task t = new Task(execute);
  t.Start();
  t.Wait();
}

private static void Execute() {
  for (int i = 0; i < 100; i++)
  {
    Console.WriteLine(i);
  }
}
```

In the preceding code, the task can be initialized using a `Task` object, where `Execute` is the computational method that is executed when the `Start` method is called. The `Start` method tells the .NET Core that the task can start and returns immediately. It forks the program execution into two threads that run concurrently. The first thread is the actual application thread and the second one is the one that executes the `execute` method. We have used the `t.Wait` method to wait for the worker task to show the result on the console. Otherwise, once the program exits the block of code under the `Main` method, the application ends.

The goal of parallel programming is to effectively use multiple cores. For example, we are running the preceding code in a single-core processor. These two threads will run and share the same processor. However, if the same program can run on a multi-core processor, it can run on multiple cores by utilizing each core separately, increasing the performance and achieving true parallelism:

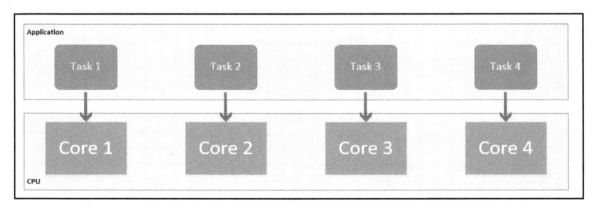

Unlike TPL, the classic `Thread` object doesn't guarantee that your thread will be running on distinct cores of the CPU. With TPL, however, it guarantees that each thread will run on the distinct thread unless it reaches the number of tasks as per the CPU and shares the cores.

To learn more about what TPL provides, please refer to
https://docs.microsoft.com/en-us/dotnet/standard/parallel-programming/task-parallel-library-tpl.

How releasing builds increases performance

Release and debug builds are two build modes provided in .NET applications. Debug mode is mostly used when we are in the process of writing code or troubleshooting errors, whereas release build mode is often used while packaging the application to deploy on production servers. When developing the deployment package, developers often miss updating the build mode to the release build, and then they face performance issues when the application is deployed:

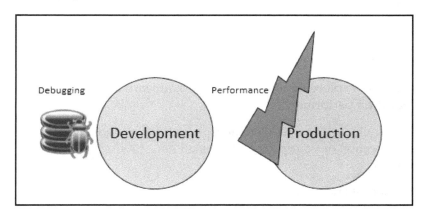

The following table shows some differences between the debug and release modes:

Debug	Release
No optimization of code is done by the compiler	Code is optimized and minified in size when built using release mode
Stack trace is captured and thrown at the time of exception	No stack trace is captured
The debug symbols are stored	All code and debug symbols under #debug directives are removed
More memory is used by the source code at runtime	Less memory is used by the source code at runtime

Benchmarking .NET Core 2.0 applications

Benchmarking applications is the process of evaluating and comparing artifacts with the agreed upon standards. To benchmark .NET Core 2.0 application code, we can use the BenchmarkDotNet tool, which provides a very simple API to evaluate the performance of code in your application. Usually, benchmarking at the micro-level, such as with classes and methods, is not an easy task, and requires quite an effort to measure the performance, whereas BenchmarkDotNet does all the low-level plumbing and the complex work associated with benchmark solutions.

Exploring BenchmarkDotNet

In this section, we will explore BenchmarkDotNet and learn how effectively it can be used to measure application performance.

It can simply be installed using a NuGet package manager console window or through the Project References section of your project. To install BenchmarkDotNet, execute the following command:

```
Install-Package BenchmarkDotNet
```

The preceding command adds a BenchmarkDotNet package from NuGet.org.

To test the BenchmarkDotNet tool, we will create a simple class that contains two methods to generate a Fibonacci series for a sequence of 10 numbers. The Fibonacci series can be implemented in multiple ways, which is why we are using it to measure which code snippet is faster and more performance efficient.

Here is the first method that generates the Fibonacci sequence iteratively:

```
public class TestBenchmark
{
  int len= 10;
  [Benchmark]
  public  void Fibonacci()
  {
    int a = 0, b = 1, c = 0;
    Console.Write("{0} {1}", a, b);

    for (int i = 2; i < len; i++)
    {
      c = a + b;
      Console.Write(" {0}", c);
```

```
        a = b;
        b = c;
    }
  }
}
```

Here is another method that uses the recursive approach to generate the Fibonacci series:

```
[Benchmark]
public  void FibonacciRecursive()
{
    int len= 10;
    Fibonacci_Recursive(0, 1, 1, len);
}

private void Fibonacci_Recursive(int a,  int b,  int counter,  int len)
{
    if (counter <= len)
    {
        Console.Write("{0} ", a);
        Fibonacci_Recursive(b, a + b, counter + 1, len);
    }
}
```

Note that both of the main methods of the Fibonacci series contain a `Benchmark` attribute. This actually tells the `BenchmarkRunner` to measure methods that contain this attribute. Finally, we can call the `BenchmarkRunner` from the main entry point of the application that measures the performance and generates a report, as shown in the following code:

```
static void Main(string[] args)
{
    BenchmarkRunner.Run<TestBenchmark>();
    Console.Read();
}
```

Once the benchmark is run, we will get the report as follows:

As well as this, it also generates files in the root folder of an application that runs the `BenchmarkRunner`. Here is the .html file that contains the information about the version of `BenchmarkDotNet` and the OS, the processor, frequency, resolution, and timer details, the .NET version (in our case, .NET Core SDK 2.0.0), host, and so on:

```
BenchmarkDotNet=v0.10.9, OS=Windows 10 Redstone 2 (10.0.15063)
Processor=Intel Core i7-4900MQ CPU 2.80GHz (Haswell), ProcessorCount=8
Frequency=2728057 Hz, Resolution=366.5613 ns, Timer=TSC
.NET Core SDK=2.0.0
  [Host]     : .NET Core 2.0.0 (Framework 4.6.00001.0), 64bit RyuJIT DEBUG  [AttachedDebugger]
  DefaultJob : .NET Core 2.0.0 (Framework 4.6.00001.0), 64bit RyuJIT
```

Method	Mean	Error	StdDev
Fibonacci	22.62 us	0.6201 us	1.8087 us
FibonacciRecursive	17.54 us	0.2192 us	0.1943 us

The table contains four columns. However, we can add more columns, which are optional by default. We can also add custom columns as well. The **Method** is the name of the method that contains the benchmark attribute, the **Mean** is the average time it takes for all the measurements to be taken (where **us** is microseconds), **Error** is the time taken to process errors, and **StdDev** is the standard deviation of the measurements.

After comparing both the methods, the `FibonacciRecursive` method is more efficient as the **Mean**, **Error**, and **StdDev** values are smaller than the `Fibonacci` method.

Other than the HTML, two more files are created, a **Comma Separated Value (CSV)** file and a **Markdown Documentation (MD)** file which contains the same information.

How it works

Benchmark generates a project at runtime for each benchmark method and builds it in release mode. It tries multiple combinations to measure the method's performance by launching that method multiple times. Once the multiple cycles are run, the report is generated, containing files and information about Benchmark.

Setting parameters

In the previous example, we tested the method with only one value. Practically, when testing an enterprise application, we want to test it with different values to estimate the method's performance.

First of all, we can define a property for each parameter, set the `Params` attribute, and specify the value(s) for which we need that method to be tested. Then we can use that property in the code. `BenchmarkRun` automatically tests that method with all of the parameters and generates the report. Here is the complete code snippet of the `TestBenchmark` class:

```
public class TestBenchmark
{

  [Params(10,20,30)]
  public int Len { get; set; }
  [Benchmark]
  public  void Fibonacci()
  {
    int a = 0, b = 1, c = 0;
    Console.Write("{0} {1}", a, b);
```

```
    for (int i = 2; i < Len; i++)
    {
      c = a + b;
      Console.Write(" {0}", c);
      a = b;
      b = c;
    }
}

[Benchmark]
public  void FibonacciRecursive()
{
  Fibonacci_Recursive(0, 1, 1, Len);
}

private void Fibonacci_Recursive(int a, int b, int counter, int len)
{
  if (counter <= len)
  {
    Console.Write("{0} ", a);
    Fibonacci_Recursive(b, a + b, counter + 1, len);
  }
}
}
```

After running Benchmark, the following report is generated:

```
BenchmarkDotNet=v0.10.9, OS=Windows 10 Redstone 2 (10.0.15063)
Processor=Intel Core i7-4900MQ CPU 2.80GHz (Haswell), ProcessorCount=8
Frequency=2728057 Hz, Resolution=366.5613 ns, Timer=TSC
.NET Core SDK=2.0.0
  [Host]     : .NET Core 2.0.0 (Framework 4.6.00001.0), 64bit RyuJIT DEBUG
  DefaultJob : .NET Core 2.0.0 (Framework 4.6.00001.0), 64bit RyuJIT
```

Method	Len	Mean	Error	StdDev
Fibonacci	10	16.35 us	0.3267 us	0.3889 us
FibonacciRecursive	10	17.69 us	0.2207 us	0.2064 us
Fibonacci	20	36.52 us	0.6865 us	0.6742 us
FibonacciRecursive	20	38.50 us	0.7291 us	0.7488 us
Fibonacci	30	59.66 us	0.8321 us	0.7377 us
FibonacciRecursive	30	65.35 us	1.2867 us	1.1406 us

Memory diagnostics using BenchmarkDotnet

With `BenchmarkDotnet`, we can also diagnose any problems with the memory and measure the number of allocated bytes and garbage collection.

It can be implemented using a `MemoryDiagnoser` attribute at the class level. To start, let's just add the `MemoryDiagnoser` attribute to the `TestBenchmark` class that we created in the last example:

```
[MemoryDiagnoser]
public class TestBenchmark {}
```

Rerun the application. Now it will collect other memory allocation and garbage collection information and generate logs accordingly:

```
BenchmarkDotNet=v0.10.9, OS=Windows 10 Redstone 2 (10.0.15063)
Processor=Intel Core i7-4900MQ CPU 2.80GHz (Haswell), ProcessorCount=8
Frequency=2728057 Hz, Resolution=366.5613 ns, Timer=TSC
.NET Core SDK=2.0.0
  [Host]     : .NET Core 2.0.0 (Framework 4.6.00001.0), 64bit RyuJIT DEBUG
  DefaultJob : .NET Core 2.0.0 (Framework 4.6.00001.0), 64bit RyuJIT
```

Method	Len	Mean	Error	StdDev	Median	Gen 0	Gen 1	Allocated
Fibonacci	10	16.50 us	0.3281 us	0.7604 us	16.37 us	0.1984	-	848 B
FibonacciRecursive	10	25.46 us	3.2510 us	9.3799 us	20.97 us	0.1984	-	880 B
Fibonacci	20	62.13 us	3.8042 us	10.8537 us	62.22 us	0.4272	0.0012	1816 B
FibonacciRecursive	20	81.60 us	15.0942 us	44.5056 us	63.55 us	0.4272	-	1848 B
Fibonacci	30	99.37 us	9.4387 us	27.3834 us	97.40 us	0.6714	-	2856 B
FibonacciRecursive	30	103.11 us	7.1130 us	20.1784 us	103.42 us	0.6714	-	2888 B

In the preceding table, the **Gen 0** and **Gen 1** columns each contain the number of that particular generation per 1,000 operations. If the value is 1, then it means that the garbage collection was done after 1,000 operations. However, note that in the first row, the value is *0.1984*, which means that the garbage collection was done after *198.4* seconds, whereas for **Gen 1** of that row, no garbage collection took place. **Allocated** represents the size of the memory that is allocated while invoking that method. It does not include the Stackalloc/heap native allocations.

Adding configurations

Benchmark configuration can be defined by creating a custom class and inheriting it from the ManualConfig class. Here is an example of the TestBenchmark class that we created earlier containing some benchmark methods:

```
[Config(typeof(Config))]
public class TestBenchmark
{
  private class Config : ManualConfig
  {
    // We will benchmark ONLY method with names with names (which
    // contains "A" OR "1") AND (have length < 3)
    public Config()
    {
      Add(new DisjunctionFilter(
        new NameFilter(name => name.Contains("Recursive"))
      ));
    }
  }

  [Params(10,20,30)]
  public int Len { get; set; }
  [Benchmark]
  public  void Fibonacci()
  {
    int a = 0, b = 1, c = 0;
    Console.Write("{0} {1}", a, b);

    for (int i = 2; i < Len; i++)
    {
      c = a + b;
      Console.Write(" {0}", c);
      a = b;
      b = c;
    }
  }

  [Benchmark]
  public  void FibonacciRecursive()
  {
    Fibonacci_Recursive(0, 1, 1, Len);
  }

  private void Fibonacci_Recursive(int a, int b, int counter, int len)
  {
    if (counter <= len)
```

```
    {
      Console.Write("{0} ", a);
      Fibonacci_Recursive(b, a + b, counter + 1, len);
    }
  }
}
```

In the preceding code, we defined the `Config` class that inherits the `ManualConfig` class provided in the benchmark framework. Rules can be defined inside the `Config` constructor. In the preceding example, there is a rule that stipulates that only those benchmark methods that contain `Recursive` should be executed. In our case, we have only one method, `FibonacciRecursive`, that will be executed and whose performance we will measure.

Another way of doing this is through the fluent API, where we can skip creating a `Config` class and implement the following:

```
static void Main(string[] args)
{
  var config = ManualConfig.Create(DefaultConfig.Instance);
  config.Add(new DisjunctionFilter(new NameFilter(
    name => name.Contains("Recursive"))));
  BenchmarkRunner.Run<TestBenchmark>(config);
}
```

To learn more about `BenchmarkDotNet`, refer to `http://benchmarkdotnet.org/Configs.htm`.

Summary

In this chapter, we have learned about the core concepts of .NET Core, including the compilation process, garbage collection, how to develop high-performant .NET Core applications by utilizing multiple cores of the CPU, and publishing an application using a release build. We have also explored the benchmarking tool, which is highly used for code optimization, and provides results specific to class objects.

In the next chapter, we will learn about multithreading and concurrent programming in .NET Core.

3
Multithreading and Asynchronous Programming in .NET Core

Multithreading and asynchronous programming are two essential techniques that facilitate the development of highly scalable and performant applications. If the application is not responsive, it affects the user experience and increases the level of dissatisfaction. On the other hand, it also increases the resource usage on the server side, or where the application is running, and also increases the memory size and/or CPU usage. Nowadays, hardware is very cheap, and every machine comes with multiple CPU cores. Implementing multithreading and using asynchronous programming techniques not only increases the performance of the application, but also makes the application more responsive in nature.

This chapter examines the core concepts of multithreading and the asynchronous programming model to help you use them in your projects and increase the overall performance of your applications.

The following is a list of the topics that we will learn about in this chapter:

- Multithreading versus asynchronous programming
- Multithreading in .NET Core
- Threads in .NET Core
- Thread synchronization
- Task parallel library (TPL)
- Creating a task using TPL
- Task-based asynchronous pattern
- Design patterns for parallel programming

I/O bound operations are code that is dependent on external resources. Examples include accessing a filesystem, accessing a network, and so on.

Multithreading versus asynchronous programming

Multithreading and asynchronous programming, if properly implemented, improve the performance of an application. Multithreading refers to the practice of executing multiple threads at the same time to execute multiple operations or tasks in parallel. There could be one main thread and several background threads, usually known as worker threads, running in parallel at the same time, executing multiple tasks concurrently, whereas both synchronous and asynchronous operations can run on a single-threaded or a multithreaded environment.

In a single-threaded synchronous operation, there is only one thread that performs all the tasks in a defined sequence, and it executes them one after the other. In a single-threaded asynchronous operation, there is only one thread that executes the tasks, but it allocates a time slice in which to run each task. When the time slice is over, it saves the state of that task and starts executing the next one. Internally, the processor performs the context switching between each task and allocates a time slice in which to run them.

In a multithreaded synchronous operation, there are multiple threads that run the tasks in parallel. There is no context switching between the tasks, like we have in an asynchronous operation. One thread is responsible for executing the tasks assigned to it and then starting another task, whereas in a multithreaded asynchronous operation, multiple threads run multiple tasks and the task can be served and executed by single or multiple threads.

The following diagram depicts the differences between the single and multithreaded synchronous and asynchronous operations:

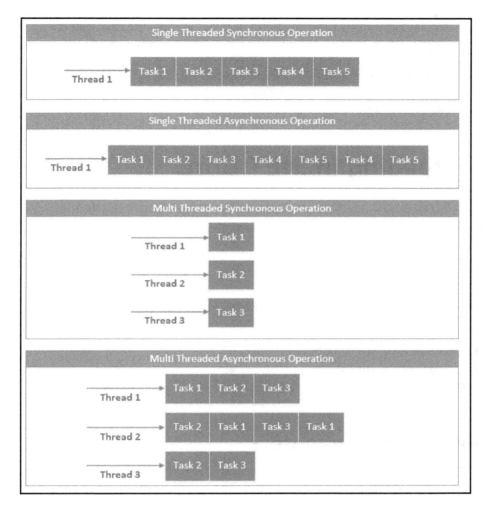

The preceding diagram shows four types of operations. In the single-threaded synchronous operation, we have one thread running five tasks sequentially. Once **Task 1** is completed, **Task 2** is executed, and so on. In the single-threaded asynchronous operation, we have a single thread, but each task will get a time slice to execute before the next task is executed and so on. Each task will be executed multiple times and resume from where it was paused. In the multi-threaded synchronous operation, we have three threads running three tasks **Task 1**, **Task 2**, and **Task 3** in parallel. Lastly, in the multithreaded asynchronous operation, we have three tasks—**Task 1**, **Task 2**, and **Task 3**—running by three threads, but each thread performs some context switching based on the time slice allocated to each task.

In asynchronous programming, it is not always the case that each asynchronous operation will be running on a new thread. Async/Await is a good example of a situation where there is no additional thread created. The *async* operation is executed in the current synchronization context of the main thread and queues the asynchronous operation executed in the allocated time slice.

Multithreading in .NET Core

There are many benefits in using multithreading in CPU and/or I/O-bound applications. It is often used for long-running processes that have a longer or infinite lifetime, working as background tasks, keeping the main thread available in order to manage or handle user requests. However, unnecessary use may completely degrade the application's performance. There are cases where creating too many threads is not a good architecture practice.

Here are some examples where multithreading is a good fit:

- I/O operations
- Running long-running background tasks
- Database operations
- Communicating over a network

Multithreading caveats

Although there are many benefits to multithreading, there are some caveats that need to be thoroughly addressed when writing multithreaded applications. If the machine is a single or two-core machine and the application is creating lots of threads, the context switching between these threads will slow the performance:

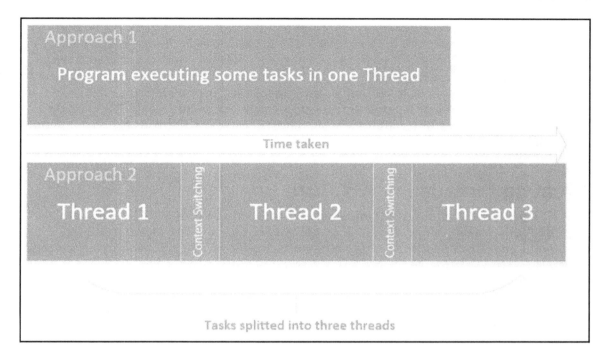

The preceding diagram depicts the program running on a single-processor machine. The first task executes synchronously, and runs comparatively faster than the three threads running on the single processor. The system executes the first thread, then waits for a while before moving on to execute the second thread, and so on. This adds an unnecessary overhead of switching between threads and, thus, delays the overall operation. In the field of threading, this is known as context switching. The boxes between each thread represent the delay occurring during each context switch between threads.

As far as the developer experience is concerned, debugging and testing are two other issues that are challenging for developers when creating a multithreaded application.

Threads in .NET Core

Every application in .NET starts with a single thread, which is the main thread. A thread is the basic unit that the operating system uses to allocate processor time. Each thread has a priority, exception handlers, and a data structure saved in its own thread context. If the exception is thrown, it is thrown inside the context of the thread and other threads are not affected by it. The thread context contains some low-level information about, for example, the CPU registers, the address space of the thread's host process, and so on.

If an application is running multiple threads on a single processor, each thread will be assigned a period of processor time and will be executed one after the other. The time slice is usually small, which makes it seem as if the threads are being executed at the same time. Once the allocated time is over, the processor moves to the other thread and the previous thread wait for the processor to become available again and execute it based on the time slice allocated. On the other hand, if the threads are running on multiple CPUs, then they may execute at the same time, but if there are other processes and threads running, the time slice will be allocated and executed accordingly.

Creating threads in .NET Core

In .NET Core, the threading API is the same as that used in the full .NET Framework version. A new thread can be created by creating a `Thread` class object and passing the `ThreadStart` or `ParameterizedThreadStart` delegate as a parameter. `ThreadStart` and `ParameterizedThreadStart` wrap a method that is invoked when the new thread is started. `ParameterizedThreadStart` is used for method containing parameters.

Here is a basic example that runs the `ExecuteLongRunningOperation` method on a separate thread:

```
static void Main(string[] args)
{
  new Thread(new ThreadStart(ExecuteLongRunningOperation)).Start();
}
static void ExecuteLongRunningOperation()
{
  Thread.Sleep(100000);
  Console.WriteLine("Operation completed successfully");
}
```

We can also pass parameters while starting the thread and use the `ParameterizedThreadStart` delegate:

```
static void Main(string[] args)
{
  new Thread(new ParameterizedThreadStart
  (ExecuteLongRunningOperation)).Start(100000);
}
static void ExecuteLongRunningOperation(object milliseconds)
{
  Thread.Sleep((int)milliseconds);
  Console.WriteLine("Operation completed successfully");
}
```

The `ParameterizedThreadStart` delegate takes an object as a parameter. So, if you want to pass multiple parameters, this can be done by creating a custom class and adding the following properties:

```
public interface IService
{
  string Name { get; set; }
  void Execute();
}

public class EmailService : IService
{
  public string Name { get; set; }
  public void Execute() => throw new NotImplementedException();

  public EmailService(string name)
  {
    this.Name = name;
  }
}

static void Main(string[] args)
{
  IService service = new EmailService("Email");
  new Thread(new ParameterizedThreadStart
  (RunBackgroundService)).Start(service);
}

static void RunBackgroundService(Object service)
{
  ((IService)service).Execute(); //Long running task
}
```

Every thread has a thread priority. When a thread is created, its priority is set to normal. The priority affects the execution of the thread. The higher the priority, the higher the precedence that will be given to the thread. The thread priority can be defined on the thread object, as follows:

```
static void RunBackgroundService(Object service)
{
  Thread.CurrentThread.Priority = ThreadPriority.Highest;
  ((IService)service).Execute(); //Long running task
}
```

`RunBackgroundService` is the method that executes in a separate thread, and the priority can be set by using the `ThreadPriority` enum and referencing the current thread object by calling `Thread.CurrentThread`, as shown in the preceding code snippet.

Thread lifetime

The lifetime of the thread depends on the method executing within that thread. Once the method is executed, CLR de-allocates the memory taken by the thread and disposes of. On the other hand, the thread can also be disposed of explicitly by calling the `Interrupt` or `Abort` methods.

Another very important factor to consider is exceptions. If the exceptions are not properly handled within a thread, they are propagated to the `calling` method and so on until they reach the `root` method in the call stack. When it reaches this point, CLR will shut down the thread if it is not handled.

For continuous or long-running threads, the shutdown process should be properly defined. One of the best approaches to smoothly shut down the thread is by using a `volatile bool` variable:

```
class Program
{

  static volatile bool isActive = true;
  static void Main(string[] args)
  {
    new Thread(new ParameterizedThreadStart
    (ExecuteLongRunningOperation)).Start(1000);
  }

  static void ExecuteLongRunningOperation(object milliseconds)
  {
    while (isActive)
    {
      //Do some other operation
      Console.WriteLine("Operation completed successfully");
    }
  }
}
```

In the preceding code, we have used the `volatile bool` variable `isActive`, that decides if the `while` loop execute or not.

The `volatile` keyword indicates that a field may be modified by multiple threads that are executing at the same time. Fields that are declared volatile are not subject to compiler optimizations that assume access by a single thread. This ensures that the most up-to-date value is present in the field at all times. To learn more about volatile, kindly refer the following URL:

https://docs.microsoft.com/en-us/dotnet/csharp/language-reference/keywords/volatile

The thread pool in .NET

CLR provides a separate thread pool that contains the list of threads to be used to execute tasks asynchronously. Each process has its own specific thread pool. CLR adds and removes threads in or from the thread pool.

To run a thread using `ThreadPool`, we can use `ThreadPool.QueueUserWorkItem`, as shown in the following code:

```
class Program
{
  static void Main(string[] args)
  {
    ThreadPool.QueueUserWorkItem(ExecuteLongRunningOperation, 1000);
    Console.Read();
  }
  static void ExecuteLongRunningOperation(object milliseconds)
  {

    Thread.Sleep((int)milliseconds);
    Console.WriteLine("Thread is executed");
  }
}
```

`QueueUserWorkItem` queues the task to be executed by the CLR in a thread that is available in the thread pool. The task queues are maintained in **First In, First Out (FIFO)** order. However, depending on the thread's availability and the task job itself, the task completion may be delayed.

Thread synchronization

In multithreaded applications, we have shared resources that are accessible by multiple threads executing simultaneously. The area where the resources are shared across multiple threads is known as the critical section. To protect these resources and provide thread-safe access, there are certain techniques that we will discuss in this section.

Let's take an example where we have a singleton class for logging a message into the filesystem. A singleton, by definition, denotes that there should only be one instance shared across multiple calls. Here is the basic implementation of a singleton pattern that is not thread-safe:

```
public class Logger
{
   static Logger _instance;

   private Logger() { }

   public Logger GetInstance()
   {
      _instance = (_instance == null ? new Logger() : _instance);
      return _instance;
   }

   public void LogMessage(string str)
   {
      //Log message into file system
   }

}
```

The preceding code is a lazy initialization singleton that creates an instance on the first call on the GetInstance method. GetInstance is the critical section and is not thread-safe. If multiple threads enter into the critical section, multiple instances will be created and the race condition will occur.

The race condition is a problem in multithreaded programming that occurs when the outcome depends on the timing of events. A race condition arises when two or more parallel tasks access a shared object.

To implement the thread-safe singleton, we can use a locking pattern. Locking ensures that only one thread can enter into the critical section, and if another thread attempts to enter, it will wait until the thread is released. Here is a modified version that enables a singleton to be thread-safe:

```
public class Logger
{

  private static object syncRoot = new object();
  static Logger _instance;

  private Logger() { }

  public Logger GetInstance()
  {
    if (_instance == null)
    {
      lock (syncRoot)
      {
        if (_instance == null)
        _instance = new Logger();
      }
    }
    return _instance;
  }

  public void LogMessage(string str)
  {
    //Log message into file system
  }
}
```

Monitors

Monitors are used to provide thread-safe access to the resource. It is applicable to multithread programming, where there are multiple threads that need access to a resource simultaneously. When multiple threads attempt to enter `monitor` to access any resource, CLR allows only one thread at a time to enter and the other threads are blocked. When the thread exits the monitor, the next waiting thread enters, and so on.

If we look into the `Monitor` class, all the methods such as `Monitor.Enter` and `Monitor.Exit` operate on object references. Similarly to `lock`, `Monitor` also provides gated access to the resource; however, a developer will have greater control in terms of the API it provides.

Here is a basic example of using `Monitor` in .NET Core:

```
public class Job
{
```

```
    int _jobDone;
    object _lock = new object();

    public void IncrementJobCounter(int number)
    {
      Monitor.Enter(_lock);
      // access to this field is synchronous
      _jobDone += number;
      Monitor.Exit(_lock);
    }

  }
```

The preceding code snippet represents a job process where multiple threads are working on certain tasks. When the task completes, they call the `IncrementJobCounter` method to increment the `_jobDone` counter.

There are certain cases where the critical section has to wait for the resources to be available. Once they are available, we want to pulse the waiting block to execute.

To help us understand, let's take an example of a running `Job` whose task is to run the jobs added by multiple threads. If no job is present, it should wait for the threads to push and start executing them immediately.

In this example, we will create a `JobExecutor` class that runs in a separate thread. Here is the code snippet of `JobExecutor`:

```
    public class JobExecutor
    {
      const int _waitTimeInMillis = 10 * 60 * 1000;
      private ArrayList _jobs = null;
      private static JobExecutor _instance = null;
      private static object _syncRoot = new object();
      //Singleton implementation of JobExecutor
      public static JobExecutor Instance
      {
        get{
        lock (_syncRoot)
        {
          if (_instance == null)
          _instance = new JobExecutor();
        }
        return _instance;
      }
    }
```

```csharp
private JobExecutor()
{
  IsIdle = true;
  IsAlive = true;
  _jobs = new ArrayList();
}
private Boolean IsIdle { get; set; }
public Boolean IsAlive { get; set; }

//Callers can use this method to add list of jobs
public void AddJobItems(List<Job> jobList)
{
  //Added lock to provide synchronous access.
  //Alternatively we can also use Monitor.Enter and Monitor.Exit
  lock (_jobs)
  {
    foreach (Job job in jobList)
    {
      _jobs.Add(job);
    }
    //Release the waiting thread to start executing the //jobs
    Monitor.PulseAll(_jobs);
  }
}
/*Check for jobs count and if the count is 0, then wait for 10 minutes by
calling Monitor.Wait. Meanwhile, if new jobs are added to the list,
Monitor.PulseAll will be called that releases the waiting thread. Once the
waiting is over it checks the count of jobs and if the jobs are there in
the list, start executing. Otherwise, wait for the new jobs */
public void CheckandExecuteJobBatch()
{
  lock (_jobs)
  {
    while (IsAlive)
    {
      if (_jobs == null || _jobs.Count <= 0)
      {
        IsIdle = true;
        Console.WriteLine("Now waiting for new jobs");
        //Waiting for 10 minutes
        Monitor.Wait(_jobs, _waitTimeInMillis);
      }
      else
      {
        IsIdle = false;
        ExecuteJob();
      }
    }
```

```
    }
  }

  //Execute the job
  private void ExecuteJob()
  {
    for(int i=0;i< _jobs.Count;i++)
    {
      Job job = (Job)_jobs[i];
      //Execute the job;
      job.DoSomething();
      //Remove the Job from the Jobs list
      _jobs.Remove(job);
      i--;
    }
  }
}
```

It's a singleton class, and other threads can access the JobExecutor instance using the static Instance property and call the AddJobsItems method to add the list of jobs to be executed. The CheckandExecuteJobBatch method runs continuously and checks for new jobs in the list every 10 minutes. Or, if it is interrupted by the AddJobsItems method by calling the Monitor.PulseAll method, it will immediately move to the while statement and check for the items count. If the items are present, the CheckandExecuteJobBatch method calls the ExecuteJob method that runs that job.

Here is the code snippet of the Job class containing two properties, namely JobID and JobName, and the DoSomething method that will print the JobID on the console:

```
public class Job
{
  // Properties to set and get Job ID and Name
  public int JobID { get; set; }
  public string JobName { get; set; }
  //Do some task based on Job ID as set through the JobID
  //property
  public void DoSomething()
  {
    //Do some task based on Job ID
    Console.WriteLine("Executed job " + JobID);
  }
}
```

Finally, on the main Program class, we can invoke three worker threads and one thread for JobExecutor, as shown in the following code:

```
class Program
{
  static void Main(string[] args)
  {
    Thread jobThread = new Thread(new ThreadStart(ExecuteJobExecutor));
    jobThread.Start();

    //Starting three Threads add jobs time to time;
    Thread thread1 = new Thread(new ThreadStart(ExecuteThread1));
    Thread thread2 = new Thread(new ThreadStart(ExecuteThread2));
    Thread thread3 = new Thread(new ThreadStart(ExecuteThread3));
    Thread1.Start();
    Thread2.Start();
    thread3.Start();

    Console.Read();
  }
  //Implementation of ExecuteThread 1 that is adding three
  //jobs in the list and calling AddJobItems of a singleton
  //JobExecutor instance
  private static void ExecuteThread1()
  {
    Thread.Sleep(5000);
    List<Job> jobs = new List<Job>();
    jobs.Add(new Job() { JobID = 11, JobName = "Thread 1 Job 1" });
    jobs.Add(new Job() { JobID = 12, JobName = "Thread 1 Job 2" });
    jobs.Add(new Job() { JobID = 13, JobName = "Thread 1 Job 3" });
    JobExecutor.Instance.AddJobItems(jobs);
  }

  //Implementation of ExecuteThread2 method that is also adding
  //three jobs and calling AddJobItems method of singleton
  //JobExecutor instance
  private static void ExecuteThread2()
  {
    Thread.Sleep(5000);
    List<Job> jobs = new List<Job>();
    jobs.Add(new Job() { JobID = 21, JobName = "Thread 2 Job 1" });
    jobs.Add(new Job() { JobID = 22, JobName = "Thread 2 Job 2" });
    jobs.Add(new Job() { JobID = 23, JobName = "Thread 2 Job 3" });
    JobExecutor.Instance.AddJobItems(jobs);
  }

  //Implementation of ExecuteThread3 method that is again
  // adding 3 jobs instances into the list and
  //calling AddJobItems to add those items into the list to execute
  private static void ExecuteThread3()
  {
```

```
        Thread.Sleep(5000);
        List<Job> jobs = new List<Job>();
        jobs.Add(new Job() { JobID = 31, JobName = "Thread 3 Job 1" });
        jobs.Add(new Job() { JobID = 32, JobName = "Thread 3 Job 2" });
        jobs.Add(new Job() { JobID = 33, JobName = "Thread 3 Job 3" });
        JobExecutor.Instance.AddJobItems(jobs);
    }

    //Implementation of ExecuteJobExecutor that calls the
    //CheckAndExecuteJobBatch to run the jobs
    public static void ExecuteJobExecutor()
    {
        JobExecutor.Instance.IsAlive = true;
        JobExecutor.Instance.CheckandExecuteJobBatch();
    }
}
```

The following is the output of running this code:

```
C:\WINDOWS\system32\cmd.exe
Now waiting for new jobs
Executed job 21
Executed job 22
Executed job 23
Executed job 11
Executed job 12
Executed job 13
Now waiting for new jobs
Executed job 31
Executed job 32
Executed job 33
Now waiting for new jobs
```

Task parallel library (TPL)

So far, we have learned some core concepts about multithreading, and have used threads to perform multiple tasks. Compared to the classic threading model in .NET, TPL minimizes the complexity of using threads and provides an abstraction through a set of APIs that helps developers to focus more on the application program instead of focusing on how the threads will be provisioned, as well as other things.

There are several benefits of using TPL over threads:

- It autoscales the concurrency to a multicore level
- It autoscales LINQ queries to a multicore level
- It handles the partitioning of the work and uses `ThreadPool` where required
- It is easy to use and reduces the complexity of working with threads directly

Creating a task using TPL

TPL APIs are available in the `System.Threading` and `System.Threading.Tasks` namespaces. They work around the task, which is a program or a block of code that runs asynchronously. An asynchronous task can be run by calling either the `Task.Run` or `TaskFactory.StartNew` methods. When we create a task, we provide a named delegate, anonymous method, or a lambda expression that the task executes.

Here is a code snippet that uses a lambda expression to execute the `ExecuteLongRunningTasks` method using `Task.Run`:

```
class Program
{
  static void Main(string[] args)
  {
    Task t = Task.Run(()=>ExecuteLongRunningTask(5000));
    t.Wait();
  }

  public static void ExecuteLongRunningTask(int millis)
  {
    Thread.Sleep(millis);
    Console.WriteLine("Hello World");
  }
}
```

In the preceding code snippet, we have executed the `ExecuteLongRunningTask` method asynchronously using the `Task.Run` method. The `Task.Run` method returns the `Task` object that can be used to further wait for the asynchronous piece of code to be executed completely before the program ends. To wait for the task, we have used the `Wait` method.

Alternatively, we can also use the `Task.Factory.StartNew` method, which is more advanced and provides more options. While calling the `Task.Factory.StartNew` method, we can specify `CancellationToken`, `TaskCreationOptions`, and `TaskScheduler` to set the state, specify other options, and schedule tasks.

TPL uses multiple cores of the CPU out of the box. When the task is executed using the TPL API, it automatically splits the task into one or more threads and utilizes multiple processors, if they are available. The decision as to how many threads will be created is calculated at runtime by CLR. Whereas a thread only has an affinity to a single processor, running any task on multiple processors needs a proper manual implementation.

Task-based asynchronous pattern (TAP)

When developing any software, it is always good to implement the best practices while designing its architecture. The task-based asynchronous pattern is one of the recommended patterns that can be used when working with TPL. There are, however, a few things to bear in mind while implementing TAP.

Naming convention

The method executing asynchronously should have the naming suffix `Async`. For example, if the method name starts with `ExecuteLongRunningOperation`, it should have the suffix `Async`, with the resulting name of `ExecuteLongRunningOperationAsync`.

Return type

The method signature should return either a `System.Threading.Tasks.Task` or `System.Threading.Tasks.Task<TResult>`. The task's return type is equivalent to the method that returns `void`, whereas `TResult` is the data type.

Parameters

The `out` and `ref` parameters are not allowed as parameters in the method signature. If multiple values need to be returned, tuples or a custom data structure can be used. The method should always return `Task` or `Task<TResult>`, as discussed previously.

Here are a few signatures for both synchronous and asynchronous methods:

Synchronous method	Asynchronous method
`Void Execute();`	`Task ExecuteAsync();`
`List<string> GetCountries();`	`Task<List<string>> GetCountriesAsync();`
`Tuple<int, string> GetState(int stateID);`	`Task<Tuple<int, string>> GetStateAsync(int stateID);`

Person GetPerson(int personID);	Task<Person> GetPersonAsync(int personID);

Exceptions

The asynchronous method should always throw exceptions that are assigned to the returning task. However, the usage errors, such as passing null parameters to the asynchronous method, should be properly handled.

Let's suppose we want to generate several documents dynamically based on a predefined templates list, where each template populates the placeholders with dynamic values and writes it on the filesystem. We assume that this operation will take a sufficient amount of time to generate a document for each template. Here is a code snippet showing how the exceptions can be handled:

```
static void Main(string[] args)
{
  List<Template> templates = GetTemplates();
  IEnumerable<Task> asyncDocs = from template in templates select
  GenerateDocumentAsync(template);
  try
  {
    Task.WaitAll(asyncDocs.ToArray());

  }catch(Exception ex)
  {
    Console.WriteLine(ex);
  }
  Console.Read();
}

private static async Task<int> GenerateDocumentAsync(Template template)
{
  //To automate long running operation
  Thread.Sleep(3000);
  //Throwing exception intentionally
  throw new Exception();
}
```

In the preceding code, we have a `GenerateDocumentAsync` method that performs a long running operation, such as reading the template from the database, populating placeholders, and writing a document to the filesystem. To automate this process, we used `Thread.Sleep` to sleep the thread for three seconds and then throw an exception that will be propagated to the calling method. The `Main` method loops the templates list and calls the `GenerateDocumentAsync` method for each template. Each `GenerateDocumentAsync` method returns a task. When calling an asynchronous method, the exception is actually hidden until the `Wait`, `WaitAll`, `WhenAll`, and other methods are called. In the preceding example, the exception will be thrown once the `Task.WaitAll` method is called, and will log the exception on the console.

Task status

The task object provides a `TaskStatus` that is used to know whether the task is executing the method running, has completed the method, has encountered a fault, or whether some other occurrence has taken place. The task initialized using `Task.Run` initially has the status of `Created`, but when the `Start` method is called, its status is changed to `Running`. When applying the TAP pattern, all the methods return the `Task` object, and whether they are using the `Task.Run` inside, the method body should be activated. That means that the status should be anything other than `Created`. The TAP pattern ensures the consumer that the task is activated and the starting task is not required.

Task cancellation

Cancellation is an optional thing for TAP-based asynchronous methods. If the method accepts the `CancellationToken` as the parameter, it can be used by the caller party to cancel a task. However, for a TAP, the cancellation should be properly handled. Here is a basic example showing how cancellation can be implemented:

```
static void Main(string[] args)
{
  CancellationTokenSource tokenSource = new CancellationTokenSource();
  CancellationToken token = tokenSource.Token;
  Task.Factory.StartNew(() => SaveFileAsync(path, bytes, token));
}

static Task<int> SaveFileAsync(string path, byte[] fileBytes,
CancellationToken cancellationToken)
{
  if (cancellationToken.IsCancellationRequested)
  {
    Console.WriteLine("Cancellation is requested...");
```

```
        cancellationToken.ThrowIfCancellationRequested
    }
    //Do some file save operation
    File.WriteAllBytes(path, fileBytes);
    return Task.FromResult<int>(0);
}
```

In the preceding code, we have a SaveFileAsync method that takes the byte array and the CancellationToken as parameters. In the Main method, we initialize the CancellationTokenSource that can be used to cancel the asynchronous operation later in the program. To test the cancellation scenario, we will just call the Cancel method of the tokenSource after the Task.Factory.StartNew method and the operation will be canceled. Moreover, when the task is canceled, its status is set to Cancelled and the IsCompleted property is set to true.

Task progress reporting

With TPL, we can use the IProgress<T> interface to get real-time progress notifications from the asynchronous operations. This can be used in scenarios where we need to update the user interface or the console app of asynchronous operations. When defining the TAP-based asynchronous methods, defining IProgress<T> in a parameter is optional. We can have overloaded methods that can help consumers to use in the case of specific needs. However, they should only be used if the asynchronous method supports them. Here is the modified version of SaveFileAsync that updates the user about the real progress:

```
static void Main(string[] args)
{
  var progressHandler = new Progress<string>(value =>
  {
    Console.WriteLine(value);
  });

  var progress = progressHandler as IProgress<string>;

  CancellationTokenSource tokenSource = new CancellationTokenSource();
  CancellationToken token = tokenSource.Token;

  Task.Factory.StartNew(() => SaveFileAsync(path, bytes,
  token, progress));
  Console.Read();

}
static Task<int> SaveFileAsync(string path, byte[] fileBytes,
CancellationToken cancellationToken, IProgress<string> progress)
```

```
  {
    if (cancellationToken.IsCancellationRequested)
    {
      progress.Report("Cancellation is called");
      Console.WriteLine("Cancellation is requested...");
    }

    progress.Report("Saving File");
    File.WriteAllBytes(path, fileBytes);
    progress.Report("File Saved");
    return Task.FromResult<int>(0);

  }
```

Implementing TAP using compilers

Any method that is attributed with the `async` keyword (for C#) or `Async` for (Visual Basic) is called an asynchronous method. The `async` keyword can be applied to a method, anonymous method, or a Lambda expression, and the language compiler can execute that task asynchronously.

Here is a simple implementation of the TAP method using the compiler approach:

```
static void Main(string[] args)
{
  var t = ExecuteLongRunningOperationAsync(100000);
  Console.WriteLine("Called ExecuteLongRunningOperationAsync method,
  now waiting for it to complete");
  t.Wait();
  Console.Read();
}

public static async Task<int> ExecuteLongRunningOperationAsync(int millis)
{
  Task t = Task.Factory.StartNew(() => RunLoopAsync(millis));
  await t;
  Console.WriteLine("Executed RunLoopAsync method");
  return 0;
}

public static void RunLoopAsync(int millis)
{
  Console.WriteLine("Inside RunLoopAsync method");
  for(int i=0;i< millis; i++)
  {
    Debug.WriteLine($"Counter = {i}");
```

```
    }
    Console.WriteLine("Exiting RunLoopAsync method");
  }
```

In the preceding code, we have the `ExecuteLongRunningOperationAsync` method, which is implemented as per the compiler approach. It calls the `RunLoopAsync` that executes a loop for a certain number of milliseconds that is passed in the parameter. The `async` keyword on the `ExecuteLongRunningOperationAsync` method actually tells the compiler that this method has to be executed asynchronously, and, once the `await` statement is reached, the method returns to the `Main` method that writes the line on a console and waits for the task to be completed. Once the `RunLoopAsync` is executed, the control comes back to `await` and starts executing the next statements in the `ExecuteLongRunningOperationAsync` method.

Implementing TAP with greater control over Task

As we know, that the TPL is centered on the `Task` and `Task<TResult>` objects. We can execute an asynchronous task by calling the `Task.Run` method and execute a `delegate` method or a block of code asynchronously and use `Wait` or other methods on that task. However, this approach is not always adequate, and there are scenarios where we may have different approaches to executing asynchronous operations, and we may use an **Event-based Asynchronous Pattern (EAP)** or an **Asynchronous Programming Model (APM)**. To implement TAP principles here, and to get the same control over asynchronous operations executing with different models, we can use the `TaskCompletionSource<TResult>` object.

The `TaskCompletionSource<TResult>` object is used to create a task that executes an asynchronous operation. When the asynchronous operation completes, we can use the `TaskCompletionSource<TResult>` object to set the result, exception, or state of the task.

Here is a basic example that executes the `ExecuteTask` method that returns `Task`, where the `ExecuteTask` method uses the `TaskCompletionSource<TResult>` object to wrap the response as a `Task` and executes the `ExecuteLongRunningTask` through the `Task.StartNew` method:

```
    static void Main(string[] args)
    {
      var t = ExecuteTask();
      t.Wait();
      Console.Read();
    }
```

```
public static Task<int> ExecuteTask()
{
  var tcs = new TaskCompletionSource<int>();
  Task<int> t1 = tcs.Task;
  Task.Factory.StartNew(() =>
  {
    try
    {
      ExecuteLongRunningTask(10000);
      tcs.SetResult(1);
    }catch(Exception ex)
    {
      tcs.SetException(ex);
    }
  });
  return tcs.Task;

}

public static void ExecuteLongRunningTask(int millis)
{
  Thread.Sleep(millis);
  Console.WriteLine("Executed");
}
```

Design patterns for parallel programming

There are various ways in which the tasks can be designed to run in parallel. In this section, we will learn some top design patterns used in TPL:

- Pipeline pattern
- Dataflow pattern
- Producer-consumer pattern
- Parallel.ForEach
- Parallel LINQ (PLINQ)

Pipeline pattern

The pipeline pattern is commonly used in scenarios where we need to execute the asynchronous tasks in sequence:

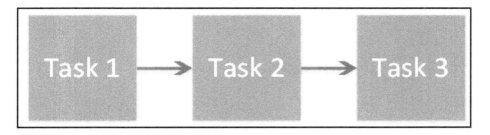

Consider a task where we need to create a user record first, then initiate a workflow and send an email. To implement this scenario, we can use the ContinueWith method of TPL. Here is a complete example:

```
static void Main(string[] args)
{

  Task<int> t1 = Task.Factory.StartNew(() =>
  { return CreateUser(); });

  var t2=t1.ContinueWith((antecedent) =>
  { return InitiateWorkflow(antecedent.Result); });
  var t3 = t2.ContinueWith((antecedant) =>
  { return SendEmail(antecedant.Result); });

  Console.Read();


}

public static int CreateUser()
{
  //Create user, passing hardcoded user ID as 1
  Thread.Sleep(1000);
  Console.WriteLine("User created");
  return 1;
}

public static int InitiateWorkflow(int userId)
{
  //Initiate Workflow
  Thread.Sleep(1000);
  Console.WriteLine("Workflow initiates");

  return userId;
}
```

```
public static int SendEmail(int userId)
{
  //Send email
  Thread.Sleep(1000);
  Console.WriteLine("Email sent");

  return userId;
}
```

Dataflow pattern

The dataflow pattern is a generalized pattern with a one-to-many and a many-to-one relationship. For example, the following diagram represents two tasks, **Task 1** and **Task 2**, that execute in parallel, and a third task, **Task 3**, that will only start when both of the first two tasks are completed. Once **Task 3** is completed, **Task 4** and **Task 5** will be executed in parallel:

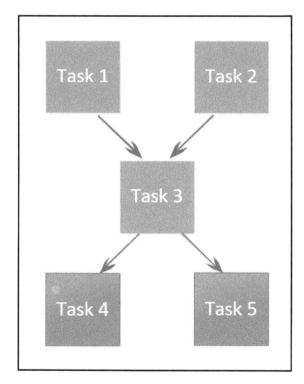

We can implement the preceding example using the following code:

```
static void Main(string[] args)
{
  //Creating two tasks t1 and t2 and starting them at the same //time
  Task<int> t1 = Task.Factory.StartNew(() => { return Task1(); });
  Task<int> t2 = Task.Factory.StartNew(() => { return Task2(); });

  //Creating task 3 and used ContinueWhenAll that runs when both the
  //tasks T1 and T2 will be completed
  Task<int> t3 = Task.Factory.ContinueWhenAll(
  new[] { t1, t2 }, (tasks) => { return Task3(); });

  //Task 4 and Task 5 will be started when Task 3 will be completed.
  //ContinueWith actually creates a continuation of executing tasks
  //T4 and T5 asynchronously when the task T3 is completed
  Task<int> t4 = t3.ContinueWith((antecendent) => { return Task4(); });
  Task<int> t5 = t3.ContinueWith((antecendent) => { return Task5(); });
  Console.Read();
}
//Implementation of Task1
public static int Task1()
{
  Thread.Sleep(1000);
  Console.WriteLine("Task 1 is executed");
  return 1;
}

//Implementation of Task2
public static int Task2()
{
  Thread.Sleep(1000);
  Console.WriteLine("Task 2 is executed");
  return 1;
}
//Implementation of Task3
public static int Task3()
{
  Thread.Sleep(1000);
  Console.WriteLine("Task 3 is executed");
  return 1;
}
Implementation of Task4
public static int Task4()
{
  Thread.Sleep(1000);
  Console.WriteLine("Task 4 is executed");
  return 1;
}
```

```
//Implementation of Task5
public static int Task5()
{
  Thread.Sleep(1000);
  Console.WriteLine("Task 5 is executed");
  return 1;
}
```

Producer/consumer pattern

One of the best patterns to execute long-running operations is the producer/consumer pattern. In this pattern, there are producers and consumers, and one or more producers are connected to one or more consumers through a shared data structure known as BlockingCollection. BlockingCollection is a fixed-sized collection used in parallel programming. If the collection is full, the producers are blocked, and if the collection is empty, no more consumers should be added:

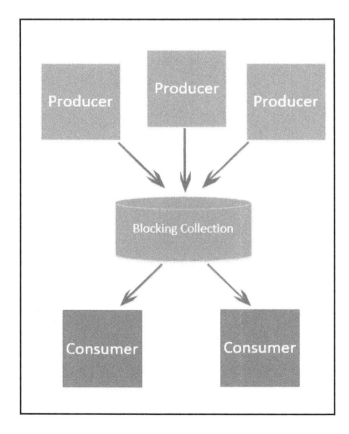

In a real-world example, the producer could be a component reading images from a database and the consumer could be a component that processes that image and saves it into a filesystem:

```
static void Main(string[] args)
{
  int maxColl = 10;
  var blockingCollection = new BlockingCollection<int>(maxColl);
  var taskFactory = new TaskFactory(TaskCreationOptions.LongRunning,
  TaskContinuationOptions.None);

  Task producer = taskFactory.StartNew(() =>
  {
    if (blockingCollection.Count <= maxColl)
    {
      int imageID = ReadImageFromDB();
      blockingCollection.Add(imageID);
      blockingCollection.CompleteAdding();
    }
  });


  Task consumer = taskFactory.StartNew(() =>
  {
    while (!blockingCollection.IsCompleted)
    {
      try
      {
        int imageID = blockingCollection.Take();
        ProcessImage(imageID);
      }
      catch (Exception ex)
      {
        //Log exception
      }
    }
  });

  Console.Read();

}

public static int ReadImageFromDB()
{
  Thread.Sleep(1000);
  Console.WriteLine("Image is read");
  return 1;
```

```
}

public static void ProcessImage(int imageID)
{
  Thread.Sleep(1000);
  Console.WriteLine("Image is processed");
}
```

In the preceding example, we initialized the generic `BlockingCollection<int>` to store the `imageID` that will be added by the producer and processed through the consumer. We set the maximum size of the collection to 10. Then, we added a `Producer` item that reads the image from a database and calls the `Add` method to add the `imageID` in the blocking collection, which can be further picked up and processed by the consumer. The consumer task just checks any available item in the collection and processes it.

 To learn more about the data structures available for parallel programming, please refer to `https://docs.microsoft.com/en-us/dotnet/standard/parallel-programming/data-structures-for-parallel-programming`.

Parallel.ForEach

The `Parallel.ForEach` is a multithreaded version of the classic `foreach` loop. The `foreach` loop runs on a single thread, whereas the `Parallel.ForEach` runs on multiple threads and utilizes multiple cores of the CPU, if available.

Here is a basic example using `Parallel.ForEach` on a list of documents that needs to be processed, and which contains an I/O-bound operation:

```
static void Main(string[] args)
{
  List<Document> docs = GetUserDocuments();
  Parallel.ForEach(docs, (doc) =>
  {
    ManageDocument(doc);
  });
}
private static void ManageDocument(Document doc) => Thread.Sleep(1000);
```

To replicate the I/O-bound operation, we just added a delay of 1 second to the `ManageDocument` method. If you execute the same method using the `foreach` loop, the difference will be obvious.

Parallel LINQ (PLINQ)

Parallel LINQ is a version of LINQ that executes queries in parallel on multi-core CPUs. It contains the full set of standard LINQ query operators plus some additional operators for parallel operations. It is highly advisable that you use this for long-running tasks, although incorrect use may slow down the performance of your app. Parallel LINQ operates on collections such as `List`, `List<T>`, `IEnumerable`, `IEnumerable<T>` and so on. Under the hood, it splits the list into segments and runs each segment on a different processor of the CPU.

Here is a modified version of the previous example, with `Parallel.ForEach` instead of the PLINQ operation:

```
static void Main(string[] args)
{
  List<Document> docs = GetUserDocuments();

  var query = from doc in docs.AsParallel()
  select ManageDocument(doc);
}

private static Document ManageDocument(Document doc)
{
  Thread.Sleep(1000);
  return doc;
}
```

Summary

In this chapter, we have learned about the core fundamentals of multithreaded and asynchronous programming. The chapter starts with the basic differences between both and walks you through some core concepts about multithreading, what APIs there are available, and how to write multithreading applications. We also looked at how the task-programming library can be used to serve asynchronous operations and how to implement the task asynchronous pattern. Finally, we explored parallel programming techniques and some of the best design patterns that are used for these techniques.

In the next chapter, we will explore the types of data structures and their impact on performance, how to write optimized code, and some best practices.

4
Data Structures and Writing Optimized Code in C#

Data structures are a particular way of storing data in software engineering. They play a vital role in storing data in a computer so that it can be accessed and modified efficiently, and they provide different storing mechanisms for storing different types of data. There are many types of data structure, and each one is designed to store a definite type of data. In this chapter, we will cover data structures in detail and learn which data structures should be used for particular scenarios in order to improve the performance of the system as regards data storage and retrieval. We will also learn how we can write optimized code in C# and what primary factors can affect performance, which is sometimes overlooked by developers when coding programs. We will learn some best practices that can be used to optimize code that is performance effective.

In this chapter, we will cover the following topics:

- What data structures are and their characteristics
- Choosing the right data structure for performance optimizations
- Understand the use of Big O notation to measure the performance and complexity of a program
- Best practices when writing code in .NET Core

What are data structures?

A data structure is a way of storing and unifying data in such a way that operations on that data can be performed in an efficient manner. The data can be stored in several ways. For example, we can have a `Person` object that contains a few properties, such as `PersonID` and `PersonName`, where `PersonID` is of the integer type and `PersonName` is of the *string* type. This `Person` object stores the data in memory, and can be further used to save that record in the database. Another example is an array called `Countries` of the `string` type that contains a list of countries. We can use the `Countries` array to retrieve a country name and use it in a program. Therefore, any type of object that stores data is called a data structure. All primitive types, such as integers, strings, chars, and Booleans, are different types of data structure, whereas other collection types, such as `LinkedList`, `ArrayList`, `SortedList`, and others, are also types of data structure that can store information in exclusive ways.

The following diagram illustrates the types of data structures and their relationship to each other:

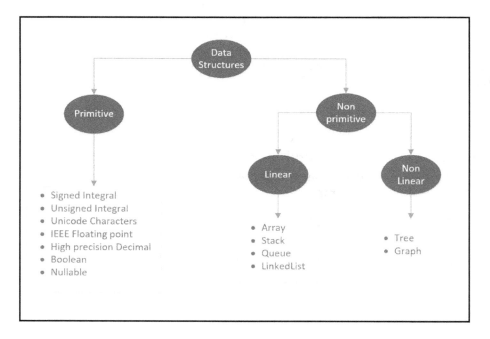

There are two types of data structure: *primitive* and *nonprimitive* types. Primitive types are value types that include *signed integral, unsigned integral, unicode characters, IEEE floating point, high-precision decimal, Boolean, enum, struct* and *nullable* value types.

Here is a list of the primitive data types available in C#:

Primitive types	
Signed integral	`sbyte, short, int, long`
Unsigned integral	`byte, ushort, uint, ulong`
Unicode characters	`Char`
IEEE floating point	`float, double`
High-precision decimal	`Decimal`
Boolean	`Bool`
String	`String`
Object	`System.Object`

Nonprimitive types are user-defined types, and further categorized as linear or nonlinear types. In a linear data structure, the elements are organized in a sequence, such as in *Array, Linked List,* and other related types, whereas in a nonlinear data structure, the elements are stored without any sequence, such as in *trees* and *graphs.*

The following table shows the types of linear and nonlinear classes available in .NET Core:

Nonprimitive types - linear data structures	
Array	`ArrayList, String[], primitive typed arrays, List, Dictionary, Hashtable, BitArray`
Stack	`Stack<T>, SortedSet<T>, SynchronizedCollection<T>`
Queue	`Queue<T>`
Linked list	`LinkedList<T>`

.NET Core does not provide any nonprimitive, nonlinear types to represent data in tree or graph formats. However, we can develop custom classes to support these kinds of types.

For example, here is the code to write a custom tree that stores data in the tree format:

```
class TreeNode
{
  public TreeNode(string text, object tag)
  {
    this.NodeText = text;
    this.Tag = tag;
    Nodes = new List<TreeNode>();
  }
  public string NodeText { get; set; }
  public Object Tag { get; set; }
  public List<TreeNode> Nodes { get; set; }
}
```

Finally, we can write a program to populate a tree view on the console window as follows:

```
static void Main(string[] args)
{
  TreeNode node = new TreeNode("Root", null);
  node.Nodes.Add(new TreeNode("Child 1", null));
  node.Nodes[0].Nodes.Add(new TreeNode("Grand Child 1", null));
  node.Nodes.Add(new TreeNode("Child 1 (Sibling)", null));
  PopulateTreeView(node, "");
  Console.Read();
}

//Populates a Tree View on Console
static void PopulateTreeView(TreeNode node, string space)
{
  Console.WriteLine(space + node.NodeText);
  space = space + " ";
  foreach(var treenode in node.Nodes)
  {
    //Recurive call
    PopulateTreeView(treenode, space);
  }
}
```

When you run the preceding program, it generates the following output:

```
Root
  Child 1
    Grand Child 1
  Child 1 (Sibling)
```

Understanding the use of Big O notation to measure the performance and complexity of an algorithm

Big O notation is used to define the complexity and performance of an algorithm with respect to time or space consumed during execution. It is an essential technique to express the performance of an algorithm and determine the worst-case complexity of the program.

To understand it in detail, let's go through some code examples and use Big O notation to calculate their performance.

If we calculate the complexity of the following program, the Big O notation will be equal to *O(1)*:

```
static int SumNumbers(int a, int b)
{
  return a + b;
}
```

This is because, however the parameter is specified, it is just adding and returning it.

Let's consider another program that loops through the list. The Big O notation will be determined as *O(N)*:

```
static bool FindItem(List<string> items, string value)
{
  foreach(var item in items)
  {
    if (item == value)
    {
      return true;
    }
```

```
    }
    return false;
  }
```

In the preceding example, the program is looping through the item list and comparing the value passed as a parameter with each item in the list. If the item is found, the program returns true.

The complexity is determined as *O(N)* because the worst-case scenario could be a loop towards *N* items where *N* could be either a first index or any index until it reaches the last index, which is *N*.

Now, let's look at an example of the *selection sort*, which is defined as *O(N2)*:

```
static void SelectionSort(int[] nums)
{
  int i, j, min;

  // One by one move boundary of unsorted subarray
  for (i = 0; i <nums.Length-1; i++)
  {
    min = i;
    for (j = i + 1; j < nums.Length; j++)
    if (nums[j] < nums[min])
    min = j;

    // Swap the found minimum element with the first element
    int temp = nums[min];
    nums[min] = nums[i];
    nums[i] = temp;
  }
}
```

In the preceding example, we have two loops that are nested. The first loop traverses from 0 to the last index, whereas the second loop traverses from the next item to the penultimate item and swaps the values to sort the array in ascending order. The number of nested loops is directly proportional to the power of *N*, hence the Big O notation is defined as *O(N2)*.

Next, let's consider a recursive function where the Big O notation is defined as *O(2N)*, where *2N* determines the time taken, which doubles with each additional element in the input dataset that runs for an exponential period of time. Here is an example of a Fibonacci_Recursive method that recursively calls the method until the counter becomes equal to the maximum number:

```
static void Main(string[] args){
  Fibonacci_Recursive(0, 1, 1, 10);
```

```
}

static void Fibonacci_Recursive(int a, int b, int counter, int maxNo)
{
    if (counter <= maxNo)
    {
        Console.Write("{0} ", a);
        Fibonacci_Recursive(b, a + b, counter + 1, len);
    }
}
```

Logarithms

A logarithm operation is the complete opposite of an exponential operation. The logarithm is a quantity representing the power to which a base number must be raised to produce a given number.

For example, *2x = 32*, where *x=5*, can be represented as *log2 32 =5*.

In this case, the logarithm of above expression is 5 that represents the power of a fixed number 2 which is raised to produce a given number 32.

Consider a binary search algorithm that works more effectively by splitting the list of an item into two datasets and uses a specific dataset based on the number. For example, say that I have a list of different numbers sorted in ascending order:

{1, 5, 6, 10, 15, 17, 20, 42, 55, 60, 67, 80, 100}

Say that we want to find number *55*. One way to do this is to loop through each index and check each item one by one. The more effective way is to split the list into two sets and check whether the number I am looking for is greater than the last item of the first dataset or to use the second dataset.

Here is an example of a binary search whose Big O notation will be determined as *O(LogN)*:

```
static int binarySearch(int[] nums, int startingIndex, int length, int
itemToSearch)
{
    if (length >= startingIndex)
    {
        int mid = startingIndex + (length - startingIndex) / 2;

        // If the element found at the middle itself
        if (nums[mid] == itemToSearch)
        return mid;
```

```
      // If the element is smaller than mid then it is
      // present in left set of array
      if (nums[mid] > itemToSearch)
      return binarySearch(nums, startingIndex, mid - 1, itemToSearch);

      // Else the element is present in right set of array
      return binarySearch(nums, mid + 1, length, itemToSearch);
   }

   // If item not found return 1
   return -1;
}
```

Choosing the right data structure for performance optimization

A data structure is a precise way of organizing data in a computer program. If data is not efficiently stored in the right data structure, it may lead to some performance issues that impact the overall experience of the application.

In this section, we will learn the advantages and disadvantages of the different collection types available in .NET Core and which ones are the better types for particular scenarios:

- Arrays and lists
- Stacks and queues
- LinkedLists (single, double, and circular)
- Dictionaries, hashtables, and hashsets
- Generic lists

Arrays

An array is a collection that holds similar types of elements. Arrays of both value types and reference types can be created.

Here are few circumstances where arrays are useful:

- If the data is of a fixed, set length, using an array is a better option as it is faster than other collections, such as `arraylists` and generic lists
- Arrays are good to represent data in a multidimensional way

- They take less memory compared to other collections
- With arrays, we can iterate through elements sequentially

The following table shows the Big O notation for each operation that can be performed in an array:

Operations	Big O notation
Access by Index	O(1)
Search	O(n)
Insert at the end	O(n)
Remove at the end	O(n)
Insert at a position before the last element	O(n)
Remove an element at an index	O(1)

As shown in the preceding table, the search for and insertion of an item in a specific position degrades performance, whereas accessing any item in an index or removing it from any position has a lower impact on performance.

Lists

Lists are extensively used by .NET developers. Although it is preferable to use it in many scenarios, there are some performance limitations, too.

Using lists is mostly advisable when you want to access the item using its index. Unlike a linked list, where you have to iterate over each node using an enumerator to search for the item, with a list, we can easily access it using an index.

Here are few recommendations where lists are useful:

- It is recommended that you use list when the collection size is not known. Resizing arrays is an expensive operation, and with lists we can easily grow the size of the collection by just adding to it as needed.
- Unlike arrays, lists do not reserve the total memory address space for the number of items when it is created. This is because, with lists, specifying the size of the collection is not needed. On the other hand, arrays depend on the type and the size at which it is initialized, and reserve the address space during initialization.

- With lists, we can use lambda expressions to filter out records, sort items in descending order, and execute other operations. Arrays do not provide sorting, filtering, or other such operations.
- Lists represent a single dimension collection.

The following table shows the Big O notation for each operation that can be performed on lists:

Operations	Big O notation
Access by index	$O(1)$
Search	$O(n)$
Insert at the end	$O(1)$
Remove from the end	$O(1)$
Insert at a position before the last element	$O(n)$
Remove an element at an index	$O(n)$

Stacks

Stacks maintain a collection of items in **Last In First Out (LIFO)** order. The last item to be inserted is retrieved first. Only two operations are allowed on stacks, namely push and pop. The real application of a stack is an undo operation that inserts the changes into the stack and, on undoing, removes the last action that was performed:

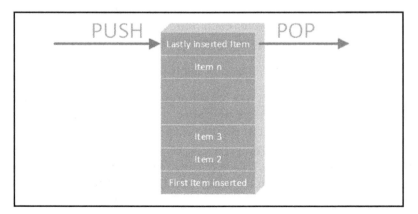

The preceding diagram illustrates how the items are added to the stack. The last inserted item pops out first, and to access the first item that was inserted, we have to pop out each element until it reaches the first one.

Here are a few of the circumstance where stacks are useful:

- Scenarios where the item should be removed when its value is accessed
- Where an undo operation needs to be implemented in a program
- To maintain navigation history on a web application
- Recursive operations

The following table shows the Big O notation for each operation that can be performed on stacks:

Operations	Big O notation
Access to the first object	$O(1)$
Search	$O(n)$
Push item	$O(1)$
Pop item	$O(1)$

Queue

Queues maintain a collection of items in a **First In First Out** (**FIFO**) order. The item inserted into the queue first is retrieved first from the queue. Only three operations are allowed in queues, namely Enqueue, Dequeue, and Peek.

Enqueue adds an element to the end of the queue, whereas Dequeue removes the element from the start of the queue. Peek returns the oldest elements in the queue but does not remove them:

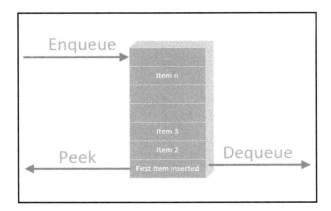

The preceding diagram illustrates how items are added to the queue. The item inserted first will be removed first from the queue and the pointer moves to the next item in the queue. Peek always returns the first item that was inserted or the item to which the pointer is set, based on whether the first item is removed.

Here are some of the circumstances where queues are useful:

- To process items in a sequence
- To serve an order based on a first-come-first-served basis

The following table shows the Big O notation for each operation that can be performed on queues:

Operations	Big O notation
Access to the first object inserted	*O(1)*
Search	*O(n)*
Queue item	*O(1)*
Enqueue item	*O(1)*
Peek item	*O(1)*

Linked lists

The linked list is a linear data structure where each node in the list contains the reference pointer to the next node, and the last node has a reference to null. The first node is known as the head. There are three types of linked list, known as *singly,* *doubly,* and *circular* linked lists.

Singly linked lists

Singly linked lists contain only the reference to the next node. The following diagram represents the singly linked list:

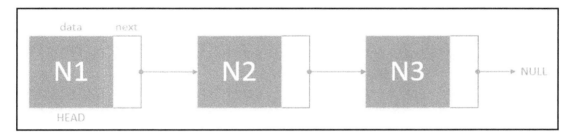

Doubly linked lists

In doubly linked lists, the nodes contain the references of both the next node and the previous node. The user can iterate forward and backward using reference pointers. The following image is a representation of a doubly linked list:

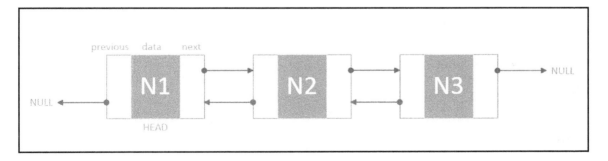

Circular linked lists

In circular linked lists, the last node points back to the first node. Here is a representation of a circular linked list:

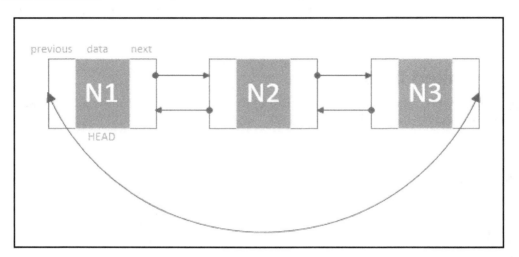

Here are a few circumstances where a linked list is useful:

- To provide access to an item in a sequential manner
- Insert an item in any position of the list
- Remove any item at any point or node
- When you need to consume less memory, as there is no array copy in the linked list

The following table shows the Big O notation value for each operation that can be performed on linked lists:

Operations	Big O notation
Access the item	O(1)
Search for the item	O(n)
Insert item	O(1)
Delete item	O(1)

Dictionaries, hashtables, and hashsets

Dictionary, hashtable, and hashset objects store items in key—value format. However, hashsets and dictionaries are good for scenarios where performance is key. Here are a few circumstances where these types are useful:

- To store an item in key–value format that can be retrieved based on a particular key
- To store unique values

The following table shows the Big O notation value for each operation that can be performed on these objects:

Operations	Big O notation
Access	*O(n)*
Search for the value if the key is not known	*O(n)*
Insert item	*O(n)*
Delete item	*O(n)*

Generic lists

The generic list is a strongly typed list of elements that is accessed using an index. In contrast to arrays, generic lists are expandable, and the list can grow dynamically; for this reason, they are known as dynamics arrays or vectors. Unlike arrays, generic lists are one dimensional, and are one of the best options for manipulating an in-memory collection of elements.

We can define a generic list as shown in the following code example. The code phrase lstNumbers allows only integer values to be stored, the phrase lstNames stores the only string, personLst stores Person objects, and so on:

```
List<int> lstNumbers = new List<int>();
List<string> lstNames = new List<string>();
List<Person> personLst = new List<Person>();
HashSet<int> hashInt = new HashSet<int>();
```

The following table shows the Big O notation value for each operation that can be performed on these objects:

Operations	Big O notation
Access by index	*O(1)*
Search	*O(n)*
Insert at the end	*O(1)*
Remove from the end	*O(1)*
Insert at a position before the last element	*O(n)*
Remove an element at an index	*O(n)*

Best practices in writing optimized code in C#

There are many factors that negatively impact the performance of a .NET Core application. Sometimes these are minor things that were not considered earlier at the time of writing the code, and are not addressed by the accepted best practices. As a result, to solve these problems, programmers often resort to ad hoc solutions. However, when bad practices are combined together, they produce performance issues. It is always better to know the best practices that help developers write cleaner code and make the application performant.

In this section, we will learn, the following topics:

- Boxing and unboxing overhead
- String concatenation
- Exceptions handling
- `for` versus `foreach`
- Delegates

Boxing and unboxing overhead

The boxing and unboxing methods are not always good to use and they negatively impact the performance of mission-critical applications. Boxing is a method of converting a value type to an object type, and is done implicitly, whereas unboxing is a method of converting an object type back to a value type and requires explicit casting.

Let's go through an example where we have two methods executing a loop of 10 million records, and in each iteration, they are incrementing the counter by 1. The `AvoidBoxingUnboxing` method is using a primitive integer to initialize and increment it on each iteration, whereas the `BoxingUnboxing` method is boxing by assigning the numeric value to the object type first and then unboxing it on each iteration to convert it back to the integer type, as shown in the following code:

```
private static void AvoidBoxingUnboxing()
{

  Stopwatch watch = new Stopwatch();
  watch.Start();
  //Boxing
  int counter = 0;
  for (int i = 0; i < 1000000; i++)
  {
    //Unboxing
    counter = i + 1;
  }
  watch.Stop();
  Console.WriteLine($"Time taken {watch.ElapsedMilliseconds}");
}

private static void BoxingUnboxing()
{

  Stopwatch watch = new Stopwatch();
  watch.Start();
  //Boxing
  object counter = 0;
  for (int i = 0; i < 1000000; i++)
  {
    //Unboxing
    counter = (int)i + 1;
  }
  watch.Stop();
  Console.WriteLine($"Time taken {watch.ElapsedMilliseconds}");
}
```

When we run both methods, we will clearly see the differences in performance. The `BoxingUnboxing` is executed seven times slower than the `AvoidBoxingUnboxing` method, as shown in the following screenshot:

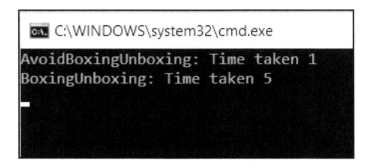

For mission-critical applications, it's always better to avoid boxing and unboxing. However, in .NET Core, we have many other types that internally use objects and perform boxing and unboxing. Most of the types under `System.Collections` and `System.Collections.Specialized` use objects and object arrays for internal storage, and when we store primitive types in these collections, they perform boxing and convert each primitive value to an object type, adding extra overhead and negatively impacting the performance of the application. Other types of `System.Data`, namely `DateSet`, `DataTable`, and `DataRow`, also use object arrays under the hood.

Types under the `System.Collections.Generic` namespace or typed arrays are the best approaches to use when performance is the primary concern. For example, `HashSet<T>`, `LinkedList<T>`, and `List<T>` are all types of generic collections.

For example, here is a program that stores the integer value in `ArrayList`:

```
private static void AddValuesInArrayList()
{

  Stopwatch watch = new Stopwatch();
  watch.Start();
  ArrayList arr = new ArrayList();
  for (int i = 0; i < 1000000; i++)
  {
    arr.Add(i);
  }
  watch.Stop();
  Console.WriteLine($"Total time taken is
  {watch.ElapsedMilliseconds}");
}
```

Let's write another program that uses a generic list of the integer type:

```
private static void AddValuesInGenericList()
{

  Stopwatch watch = new Stopwatch();
  watch.Start();
  List<int> lst = new List<int>();
  for (int i = 0; i < 1000000; i++)
  {
    lst.Add(i);
  }
  watch.Stop();
  Console.WriteLine($"Total time taken is
  {watch.ElapsedMilliseconds}");
}
```

When running both programs, the differences are pretty noticeable. The code with the generic list `List<int>` is over 10 times faster than the code with `ArrayList`. The result is as follows:

```
Total time taken with ArrayList is 63
Total time taken with List<int> is 6
```

String concatenation

In .NET, strings are immutable objects. Two strings refer to the same memory on the heap until the string value is changed. If any of the string is changed, a new string is created on the heap and is allocated a new memory space. Immutable objects are generally thread safe and eliminate the race conditions between multiple threads. Any change in the string value creates and allocates a new object in memory and avoids producing conflicting scenarios with multiple threads.

For example, let's initialize the string and assign the `Hello World` value to the a string variable:

```
String a = "Hello World";
```

Now, let's assign the a string variable to another variable, b:

```
String b = a;
```

Both a and b point to the same value on the heap, as shown in the following diagram:

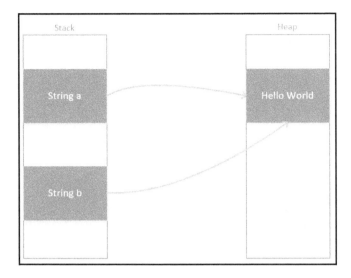

Now, suppose we change the value of b to Hope this helps:

```
b= "Hope this helps";
```

This will create another object on the heap, where a points to the same and b refers to the new memory space that contains the new text:

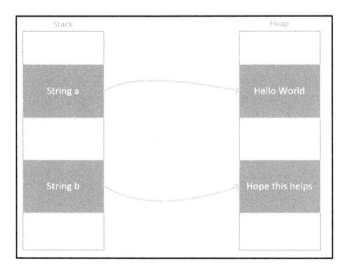

With each change in the string, the object allocates a new memory space. In some cases, it may be an overkill scenario, where the frequency of string modification is higher and each modification is allocated a separate memory space, creates work for the garbage collector in collecting the unused objects and freeing up space. In such a scenario, it is highly recommended that you use the `StringBuilder` class.

Exception handling

Improper handling of exceptions also decreases the performance of an application. The following list contains some of the best practices in dealing with exceptions in .NET Core:

- Always use a specific exception type or a type that can catch the exception for the code you have written in the method. Using the `Exception` type for all cases is not a good practice.
- It is always a good practice to use `try`, `catch`, and finally `block` where the code can throw exceptions. The final block is usually used to clean up the resources, and returns a proper response that the calling code is expecting.
- In deeply nested code, don't use `try catch` block and handle it to the calling method or main method. Catching exceptions on multiple stacks slows down performance and is not recommended.
- Always use exceptions for fatal conditions that terminate the program.
- Using exceptions for noncritical conditions, such as converting the value to an integer or reading the value from an empty array, is not recommended and should be handled through custom logic. For example, converting a string value to the integer type can be done by using the `Int32.Parse` method rather than by using the `Convert.ToInt32` method and then failing at a point when the string is not represented as a digit.
- While throwing an exception, add a meaningful message so that the user knows where that exception has actually occurred rather than going through the stack trace. For example, the following code shows a way of throwing an exception and adding a custom message based on the method and class being called:

```
static string GetCountryDetails(Dictionary<string, string>
countryDictionary, string key)
{
  try
  {
    return countryDictionary[key];
  }
  catch (KeyNotFoundException ex)
```

```
    {
        KeyNotFoundException argEx = new KeyNotFoundException("
        Error occured while executing GetCountryDetails method.
        Cause: Key not found", ex);
        throw argEx;
    }
}
```

- Throw exceptions rather than returning the custom messages or error codes and handle it in the main calling method.
- When logging exceptions, always check the inner exception and read the exception message or stack trace. It is helpful, and gives the actual point in the code where the error is thrown.

For and foreach

For and foreach are two of the alternative ways of iterating over a list of items. Each of them operates in a different way. The for loop actually loads all the items of the list in memory first and then uses an indexer to iterate over each element, whereas foreach uses an enumerator and iterates until it reaches the end of the list.

The following table shows the types of collections that are good to use for `for` and `foreach`:

Type	For/Foreach
Typed array	Good for both
Array list	Better with for
Generic collections	Better with for

Delegates

Delegates are a type in .NET which hold the reference to the method. The type is equivalent to the function pointer in C or C++. When defining a delegate, we can specify both the parameters that the method can take and its return type. This way, the reference methods will have the same signature.

Here is a simple delegate that takes a string and returns an integer:

```
delegate int Log(string n);
```

Now, suppose we have a `LogToConsole` method that has the same signature as the one shown in the following code. This method takes the string and writes it to the console window:

```
static int LogToConsole(string a) { Console.WriteLine(a);
  return 1;
}
```

We can initialize and use this delegate like this:

```
Log logDelegate = LogToConsole;
logDelegate ("This is a simple delegate call");
```

Suppose we have another method called `LogToDatabase` that writes the information in the database:

```
static int LogToDatabase(string a)
{
  Console.WriteLine(a);
  //Log to database
  return 1;
}
```

Here is the initialization of the new `logDelegate` instance that references the `LogToDatabase` method:

```
Log logDelegateDatabase = LogToDatabase;
logDelegateDatabase ("This is a simple delegate call");
```

The preceding delegate is the representation of unicast delegates, as each instance refers to a single method. On the other hand, we can also create multicast delegates by assigning `LogToDatabase` to the same `LogDelegate` instance, as follows:

```
Log logDelegate = LogToConsole;
logDelegate += LogToDatabase;
logDelegate("This is a simple delegate call");
```

The preceding code seems pretty straightforward and optimized, but under the hood, it has a huge performance overhead. In .NET, delegates are implemented by a `MutlicastDelegate` class that is optimized to run unicast delegates. It stores the reference of the method to the target property and calls the method directly. For multicast delegates, it uses the invocation list, which is a generic list, and holds the references to each method that is added. With multicast delegates, each target property holds the reference to the generic list that contains the method and executes in sequence. However, this adds an overhead for multicast delegates and takes more time to execute.

Summary

In this chapter, we have learned the core concepts about data structures, the types of data structures, as well as their advantages and disadvantages, followed by the best possible scenarios in which each can be used. We also learned about the Big O notation, which is one of the core topics to consider when writing code and helps developers to identify code performance. Finally, we looked into some best practices and covered topics such as boxing and unboxing, string concatenation, exception handling, `for` and `foreach` loops, and delegates.

In the next chapter, we will learn some guidelines and best practices that could be helpful when designing .NET Core applications.

5
Designing Guidelines for .NET Core Application Performance

Architecture and design are the core foundations for any application. Conforming to the best practices and guidelines makes the application highly maintainable, performant, and scalable. Applications can vary from a web-based application, Web APIs, a server/client TCP-based messaging application, a mission-critical application, and so on. However, all of these applications should follow certain practices that benefit in various ways. In this chapter, we will learn certain practices that are common in almost all of our applications.

Here are some of the principles we will learn in this chapter:

- Coding principles:
  - Naming convention
  - Code comments
  - One class per file
  - One logic per method
- Design principles:
  - KISS (Keep It Simple, Stupid)
  - YAGNI (You Aren't Gonna Need It)
  - DRY (Don't Repeat Yourself)
  - Separation of Concerns
  - SOLID principles
  - Caching
  - Data structures
  - Communication

- Resource management
- Concurrency

Coding principles

In this section, we will cover some of the basic coding principles that help in writing quality code that improves the overall performance and scalability of the application.

Naming convention

Always use the proper naming convention in every application, starting with the solution name, which should provide meaningful information about the project you are working on. The project name specifies the layer or component part of the application. Finally, classes should be nouns or noun phrases, and methods should represent the actions.

When we create a new project in Visual Studio, the default solution name is set to what you specify for the project name. The solution name should always be different from the project name as one solution may contain multiple projects. The project name should always represent the specific part of the system. For example, suppose we are developing a messaging gateway that sends different types of messages to different parties and contains three components, namely, listener, processor, and dispatcher; the listener listens for incoming requests, the processor processes the incoming message, and the dispatcher sends the message to the destination. The naming convention could be as follows:

- Solution name: `MessagingGateway` (or any code word)
- Listener project name: `ListenerApp`
- Processor project name: `ProcessorAPI` (if it's an API)
- Dispatcher project name: `DispatcherApp`

In .NET, the naming convention we usually follow is Pascal casing for class and method names. In Pascal casing, the first character of every word is a capital letter, whereas the parameters and other variables follow Camel casing. Here is some sample code showing how casing should be used in .NET.:

```
public class MessageDispatcher
{
  public const string SmtpAddress = "smpt.office365.com";

  public void SendEmail(string fromAddress, string toAddress,
```

```
    string subject, string body)
    {

    }
}
```

In the preceding code, we have a constant field, `SmtpAddress`, and a `SendEmail` method that is cased using Pascal casing, whereas the parameters are cased using Camel casing.

The following table summarizes the naming conventions for different artifacts in .NET:

Attribute	Naming Convention	Example
Class	Pascal casing	`class PersonManager {}`
Method	Pascal casing	`void SaveRecord(Person person) {}`
Parameters/Member variables	Camel casing	`bool isActive;`
Interface	Pascal casing; starts with letter I	`IPerson`
Enum	Pascal casing	`enum Status {InProgress, New, Completed}`

Code comments

Any code that contains proper comments assists developers in many ways. It not only reduces the time to understand the code thoroughly, but can also give leverage with certain tools like *Sandcastle* or *DocFx* to generate complete code documentation on the fly that can be shared with other developers across the team. Also, when talking about APIs, Swagger is widely used and popular in the developer community. Swagger empowers API consumers by providing complete information about the API, available methods, parameters each method takes, and so on. Swagger also reads these comments to provide the complete documentation and interface to test any API.

One class per file

Unlike many other languages, in .NET we are not restricted to create separate files for each class. We can create one single `.cs` file and create numbers of classes inside it. Conversely, this is a bad practice and painful when working with large applications.

One logic per method

Always write methods to do one thing at a time. Let's suppose we have a method that reads the user ID from the database and then calls an API to retrieve the list of documents the user has uploaded. The best approach with this scenario is to have two separate methods, `GetUserID` and `GetUserDocuments`, to retrieve the user ID first and then the documents, respectively:

```
public int GetUserId(string userName)
{
  //Get user ID from database by passing the username
}

public List<Document> GetUserDocuments(int userID)
{
  //Get list of documents by calling some API
}
```

The benefit of this approach is that it reduces code repetition. In the future, if we wanted to change the logic of either method, we just have to change it in one place rather than replicating it everywhere and increasing the chances of error.

Design principles

Developing a clean architecture adhering to the best practices adds several benefits, and application performance is one of them. We have seen many times that the technologies used behind an application are robust and powerful, but the application's performance remains unsatisfactory or poor, which is usually because of bad architecture design and investing less time on the application's design.

In this section, we will discuss a few common design principles that should be addressed when designing and developing applications in .NET Core:

- KISS (Keep It Simple, Stupid)
- YAGNI (You Aren't Gonna Need It)
- DRY (Don't Repeat Yourself)
- Separation of Concerns
- SOLID principles
- Caching
- Data structures
- Communication

- Resource management
- Concurrency

KISS (Keep It Simple, Stupid)

Writing cleaner code and keeping it simple always helps developers understand and maintain it in the long run. Adding needless complexity in the code does not only make it less understandable, but also hard to maintain and change when required. This is what KISS states. In a software context, KISS can be considered while designing software architecture, using **Object Oriented Principles** (**OOP**), designing the database, user interfaces, integration, and so on. Adding unnecessary complexity complicates the software's design and may affect the application's maintainability and performance.

YAGNI (You Aren't Gonna Need It)

YAGNI is one of the core principles of XP (extreme programming). XP is a software methodology that contains short spans of iterations to meet customer requirements and welcomes changes when they are required or initiated by the customer. The primary goal is meeting the customer's expectation, and keeping the quality and responsiveness the customer needs. It involves pair programming and code reviews to keep the quality intact and to satisfy the customer's expectations.

YAGNI is best suited for the extreme programming methodology, which helps developers focus on the features that are part of the application's functionality or customer's requirements. Doing something extra that is not communicated to the customer or is not part of the iteration or requirement may end up needing a rework and being a waste of time.

DRY (Don't Repeat Yourself)

DRY (Don't Repeat Yourself) is also one of the core principles of writing cleaner code. It addresses the challenges developers face in big applications when they are constantly changing or extending with respect to functionality or underlying logic. As per the principle, it states that *"Every piece of knowledge must have a single dependable representation within the system."*

When writing an application, we can use abstractions and avoid repetition of code to avoid redundancy. This benefits in accommodating changes and lets developers focus on one area where the change is required. If the same code is repeated in multiple areas, changes at one place need to be done in other places as well, and this eliminates good architecture practice, thus initiating higher risks of errors and making the application code more buggy.

Separation of Concerns (SoC)

One of the core principles for developing clean architecture is **Separation of Concerns (SoC)**. This pattern states that each distinct type of work application that is performing should be built separately as a separate component with little or no tight coupling with other components. For example, if a program saves the user message into the database and then a service randomly picks up the message and chooses the winner, you can see that these are two separate operations, and this is known as Separation of Concerns. With SoC, the code is considered a separate component and any customization, if needed, can be done at one place. Reusability is another factor that helps developers change code in one place so that they can use it in multiple places. Nevertheless, testing is far easier and bugs can be secluded and fixed later in case of predicament scenarios.

SOLID principles

SOLID is a collection of 5 principles, which are listed as follows. They are common design principles that are highly used when developing software design:

- **Single Responsibility Principle (SRP)**
- **Open Closed Principle (OCP)**
- **Liskov Substitution Principle (LSP)**
- **Interface Segregation Principle (ISP)**
- **Dependency Inversion Principle (DIP)**

Single Responsibility Principle

The Single Responsibility Principle states that the class should only have one particular objective and that responsibility should be entirely encapsulated from the class. If there is any change or a new objective has to be accommodated for, a new class or interface should be created.

Applying this principle in software design makes our code maintainable and easier to understand. Architects usually follow this principle when designing software architecture, but, with the passage of time when many developers work and incorporate changes into that code/class, it becomes bloated and disaffirms the single responsibility principle, thus eventually making our code unmaintainable.

This also relates to the concepts of Cohesion and Coupling. Cohesion refers to the measure of how strongly related the responsibilities in the class are, whereas coupling refers to the degree to which each class relies on one another. We should always focus on maintaining low coupling between classes and high cohesion within the class.

Here is the basic `PersonManager` class that contains four methods, namely `GetPerson`, `SavePerson`, `LogError`, and `LogInformation`:

PersonManager	Person
GetPerson()	ID
SavePerson() LogInformation() LogError()	Name

All of these methods use the database persistence manager to read/write the record into the database. As you may have noticed, `LogError` and `LogInformation` are not highly cohesive to the `PersonManager` class, and are tightly coupled with the `PersonManager` class. If we wanted to reuse these methods in other classes, we have to use the `PersonManager` class, and changing the logic of internal logging requires this `PersonManager` class to be changed as well. Hence, `PersonManager` violates the single responsibility principle.

To fix this design, we can create a separate `LogManager` class that can be used by the `PersonManager` to log information or errors when executing operations. Here is the updated class diagram representing the associations:

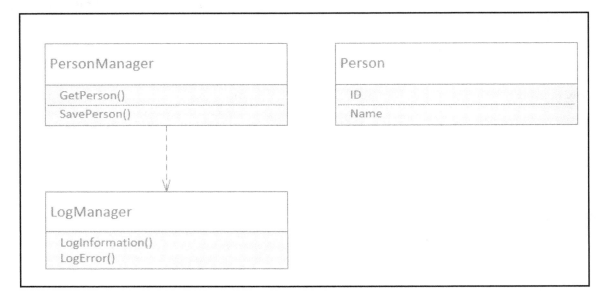

Open Closed principle

As per the definition, the Open Closed principle states that software entities like classes, methods, interfaces, and others should be closed for modification and open for extension. This means we cannot modify the existing code and extend the functionality by adding additional classes, interfaces, methods, and so on to address any changes.

Using this principle in any application solves various problems, which are listed as follows:

- Adding new functionality without changing existing code produces fewer errors and does not require thorough testing
- Less of a ripple effect that is usually experienced when changing existing code to add or update functionalities
- Extensions are mostly implemented using new interfaces or abstract classes where the existing code is unnecessary and has a lesser chance to break existing functionality

To implement the Open Closed Principle, we should use abstractions which is possible through parameters, inheritance, and composition approaches.

Parameters

Special parameters can be set in the methods, which can be used to control the behavior of the body written in that method. Suppose there is a `LogException` method that saves the exception into the database and also sends an email. Now, whenever this method is called, both the tasks will be performed. There is no way to stop sending an email for a particular exception from the code. However, if it is articulated in a way and uses some parameters to decide whether the email has to be sent out or not, it can be controlled. Nonetheless, if the existing code doesn't support this parameter, then customization is required, but, while designing, we can keep this approach to expose certain parameters so that we can handle the internal behavior of the method:

```
public void LogException(Exception ex)
{
  SendEmail(ex);
  LogToDatabase(ex);
}
```

The recommended implementation is as follows:

```
public void LogException(Exception ex, bool sendEmail, bool logToDb)
{
  if (sendEmail)
  {
    SendEmail(ex);
  }

  if (logToDb)
  {
    LogToDatabase(ex);
  }
}
```

Inheritance

With the inheritence approach, we can use the Template method pattern. Using the Template method pattern, we can create a default behavior in the root class and then create child classes to override the default behavior and implement new functionality.

For example, here is a `Logger` class that logs information into the file system:

```
public class Logger
{
  public virtual void LogMessage(string message)
  {
    //This method logs information into file system
    LogToFileSystem(message);
  }

  private void LogtoFileSystem(string message) {
    //Log to file system
  }
}
```

We have one `LogMessage` method that logs the message into the file system by calling the `LogToFileSystem` method. This method works fine until we wanted to extend the functionality. Suppose, later on, we come up with the requirement to log this information into the database as well. We have to change the existing `LogMessage` method and write the code into the same class itself. Later on, if any other requirement comes along, we have to add that functionality again and again and modify this class. As per the Open Closed Principle, this is a violation.

With the Template method pattern, we can redesign this code to follow the Open Closed Principle so that we can make it open for extension and closed for customization.

Following the OCP, here is the new design where we have one abstract class that contains the `LogMessage` abstract method, and two child classes that have their own implementations:

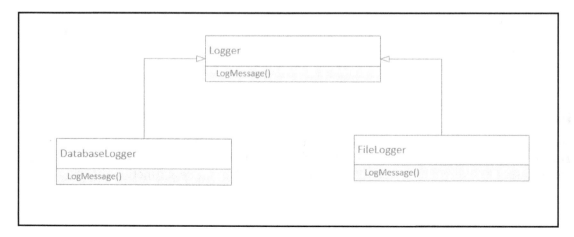

With this design, we can add the nth number of extensions without changing the existing `Logger` class:

```
public abstract class Logger
{
  public abstract void LogMessage(string message);

}

public class FileLogger : Logger
{
  public override void LogMessage(string message)
  {
    //Log to file system
  }
}

public class DatabaseLogger : Logger
{
  public override void LogMessage(string message)
  {
    //Log to database
  }
}
```

Composition

The third approach is composition, and this can be achieved using the Strategy pattern. With this approach, the client code is dependent on the abstraction, and the actual implementation is encapsulated in a separate class which is injected into the class exposed to the client.

Let's look into the following example that implements the strategy pattern. The basic requirement is to send messages that could be either emails or SMSes, and we need to construct it in a way so that new message types can be added in the future without any modification to the main class:

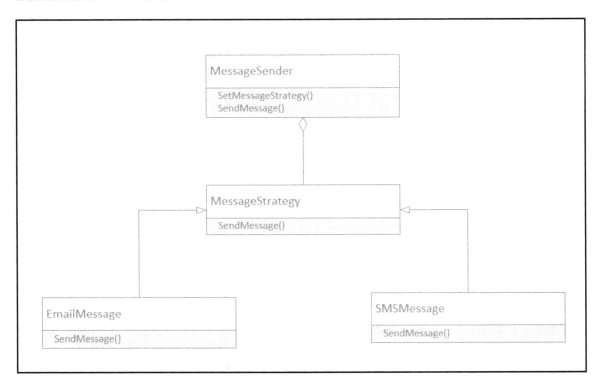

As per the strategy pattern, we have one MessageStrategy abstract class that exposes one abstract method. Each type of work is encapsulated into the separate class that inherits the MessageStrategy base abstract class.

Here is the code for the MessageStrategy abstract class:

```
public abstract class MessageStrategy
{
    public abstract void SendMessage(Message message);
}
```

We have two concrete implementations of MessageStrategy; one to send an email and another to send an SMS, which is shown as follows:

```
public class EmailMessage : MessageStrategy
{
  public override void SendMessage(Message message)
  {
    //Send Email
  }
}

public class SMSMessage : MessageStrategy
{
  public override void SendMessage(Message message)
  {
    //Send SMS
  }
}
```

Finally, we have the MessageSender class, which will be used by the client. In this class, the client can set the message strategy and call the SendMessage method that invokes the particular concrete implementation type to send the message:

```
public class MessageSender
{
  private MessageStrategy _messageStrategy;
  public void SetMessageStrategy(MessageStrategy messageStrategy)
  {
    _messageStrategy = messageStrategy;
  }

  public void SendMessage(Message message)
  {
    _messageStrategy.SendMessage(message);
  }

}
```

From the Main program, we can use MessageSender, which is shown as follows:

```
static void Main(string[] args)
{
  MessageSender sender = new MessageSender();
  sender.SetMessageStrategy(new EmailMessage());
  sender.SendMessage(new Message { MessageID = 1, MessageTo =
"jason@tfx.com",
  MessageFrom = "donotreply@tfx.com", MessageBody = "Hello readers",
```

```
    MessageSubject = "Chapter 5" });
}
```

Liskov principle

As per the Liskov principle, the function that uses the references of derived classes through the base class object must comply with the behavior of the base class.

This means that the child classes should not remove the behavior of the base class since this violates the invariants of it. Typically, the calling code should completely rely on the methods exposed in a base class without knowing its derived implementations.

Let's take an example where we first violate the definition of the Liskov principle and then fix it to learn what it is particularly designed for:

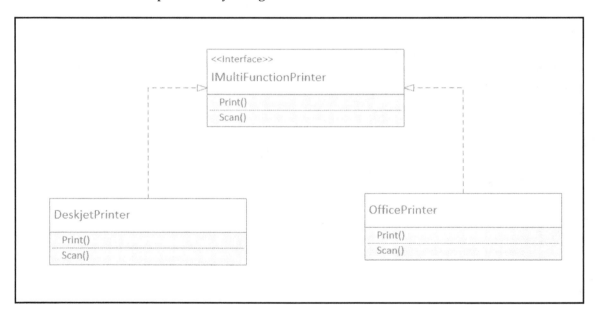

The IMultiFunctionPrinter interface exposes two methods as follows:

```
public interface IMultiFunctionPrinter
{
  void Print();
  void Scan();
}
```

This is an interface that can be implemented by different kinds of printers. The following are two kinds of printers that implement the IMultiFunctionPrinter interface, and they are as follows:

```
public class OfficePrinter: IMultiFunctionPrinter
{
  //Office printer can print the page
  public void Print() { }
  //Office printer can scan the page
  public void Scan() { }
}


public class DeskjetPrinter : IMultiFunctionPrinter
{
  //Deskjet printer print the page
  public void Print() { }
  //Deskjet printer does not contain this feature
  public void Scan() => throw new NotImplementedException();
}
```

In the preceding implementations, we have one OfficePrinter that provides printing and scanning functionalities, whereas the other home purpose DeskjetPrinter only provides the printing functionality. This DeskjetPrinter actually violates the Liskov principle as it throws the NotImplementedException when the Scan method is called.

As a remedy to the preceding problem, we can split the IMultiFunctionPrinter into two interfaces, namely IPrinter and IScanner, whereas IMultiFunctionPrinter can also implement both the interfaces to support both functionalities. The DeskjetPrinter only implements the IPrinter interface as it does not support scanning:

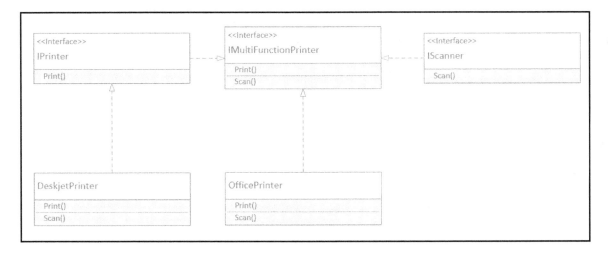

Here is the code for the three interfaces, `IPrinter`, `IScanner`, and `IMultiFunctionPrinter`:

```
public interface IPrinter
{
  void Print();
}

public interface IScanner
{
  void Scanner();
}

public interface MultiFunctionPrinter : IPrinter, IScanner
{

}
```

Finally, the concrete implementation will be as follows:

```
public class DeskjetPrinter : IPrinter
{
  //Deskjet printer print the page
  public void Print() { }
}

public class OfficePrinter: IMultiFunctionPrinter
{
  //Office printer can print the page
  public void Print() { }
```

```
    //Office printer can scan the page
    public void Scan() { }
}
```

The Interface Segregation principle

The Interface Segregation principle states that the client code should only depend on the things the client use and should not depend on anything they do not use. This means you cannot force client code to depend on certain methods which are not required.

Let's take an example that first violates the Interface Segregation principle:

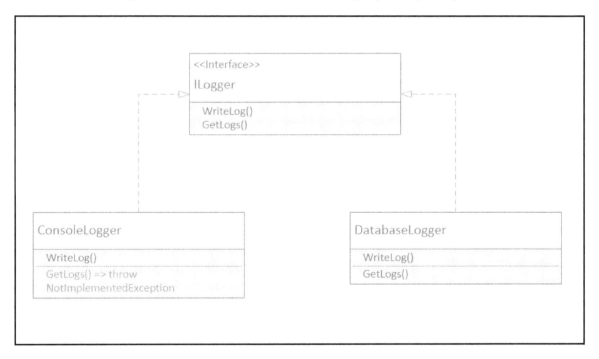

In the preceding diagram, we have the ILogger interface that contains two methods, namely `WriteLog` and `GetLogs`. The `ConsoleLogger` class writes the message into the application console window, whereas the `DatabaseLogger` class stores the message into the database. The `ConsoleLogger` prints the message on the console windows and does not persist it; it throws the `NotImplementedException` for the `GetLogs` method, and so this violates the Interface Segregation principle.

Here is the code for the preceding problem:

```
public interface ILogger
{
  void WriteLog(string message);
  List<string> GetLogs();
}

/// <summary>
/// Logger that prints the information on application console window
/// </summary>
public class ConsoleLogger : ILogger
{
  public List<string> GetLogs() => throw new NotImplementedException();
  public void WriteLog(string message)
  {
    Console.WriteLine(message);
  }
}

/// <summary>
/// Logger that writes the log into database and persist them
/// </summary>
public class DatabaseLogger : ILogger
{
  public List<string> GetLogs()
  {
    //do some work to get logs stored in database, as the actual code
    //in not written so returning null
    return null;
  }
  public void WriteLog(string message)
  {
    //do some work to write log into database
  }
}
```

To obey the **Interface Segregation Principle (ISP)**, we split the ILogger interface and make it more precise and pertinent with other implementers. The ILogger interface will only contain the WriteLog method and a new IPersistenceLogger interface is introduced that inherits the ILogger interface and provides the GetLogs method:

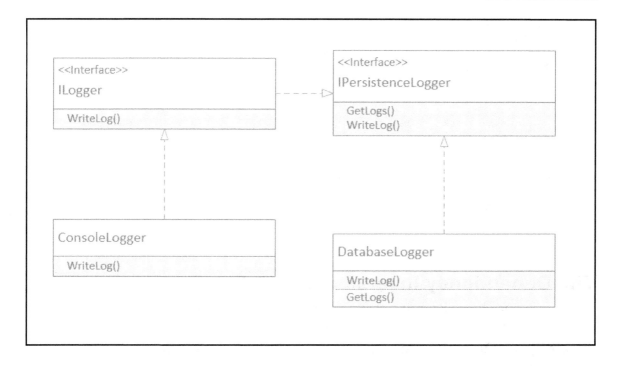

Here is the modified example, which is shown as follows:

```
public interface ILogger
{
    void WriteLog(string message);
}

public interface PersistenceLogger: ILogger
{
    List<string> GetLogs();
}

/// <summary>
/// Logger that prints the information on application console window
/// </summary>
public class ConsoleLogger : ILogger
{
    public void WriteLog(string message)
    {
        Console.WriteLine(message);
    }
}
```

```
/// <summary>
/// Logger that writes the log into database and persist them
/// </summary>
public class DatabaseLogger : PersistenceLogger
{
  public List<string> GetLogs()
  {
    //do some work to get logs stored in database, as the actual code
    //in not written so returning null
    return null;
  }
  public void WriteLog(string message)
  {
    //do some work to write log into database
  }
}
```

The Dependency Inversion principle

The Dependency Inversion principle states that high-level modules should not depend on low-level modules and both of them should depend on abstractions.

The software application contains numerous types of dependencies. A dependency could be a framework dependency, a third-party libraries dependency, a web service dependency, a database dependency, a class dependency, and so on. As per the Dependency Inversion principle, the dependencies should not be tightly coupled with one another.

For example, in the layered architecture approach we have a presentation layer where all the views are defined; the service layer that exposes certain methods used by the presentation layer; the business layer that contains core business logic of the system; and the database layer where the backend database connectors and the repository classes are defined. Consider this an ASP.NET MVC application where the controller invokes the service that references the business layer, where the business layer contains the core business logic of the system, and where it uses the database layer to perform CRUD (Create, Read, Update and Delete) operations on the database. The dependency tree will look as follows:

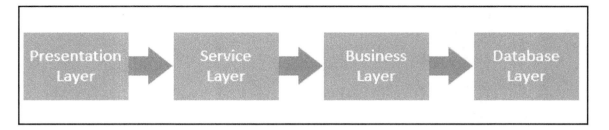

As per the Dependency Inversion principle, it is not recommended to instantiate the objects directly from each layer. This creates a tight coupling between the layers. To break this coupling, we can implement abstraction through interfaces or abstract classes. We may use some instantiation patterns like factory or dependency injection to instantiate objects. Moreover, we should always use interfaces rather than classes. Suppose in our service layer we have a reference to our business layer, and our service contract is using `EmployeeManager` to perform some CRUD operations. `EmployeeManager` contains the following methods:

```
public class EmployeeManager
{

  public List<Employee> GetEmployees(int id)
  {
    //logic to Get employees
    return null;
  }
  public void SaveEmployee(Employee emp)
  {
    //logic to Save employee
  }
  public void DeleteEmployee(int id)
  {
    //Logic to delete employee
  }

}
```

In the service layer, we can instantiate the business layer `EmployeeManager` object using the new keyword. Adding more methods in the `EmployeeManager` class will directly use the service layer based on the access modifiers being set at each method. Moreover, any changes in the existing methods will break the service layer code. If we expose the interface to the service layer and use some factory or **Dependency Injection** (**DI**) patterns, it encapsulates the underlying implementation and exposes only those methods that are needed.

The following code shows the IEmployeeManager interface being extracted from the EmployeeManager class:

```
public interface IEmployeeManager
{
  void DeleteEmployee(int id);
  System.Collections.Generic.List<Employee> GetEmployees(int id);
  void SaveEmployee(Employee emp);
}
```

Considering the preceding example, we can inject types using dependency injection, so whenever the service manager is invoked, the business manager instance will be initialized.

Caching

Caching is one of the best practices that can be used to increase application performance. It is often used with data where changes are less frequent. There are many caching providers available that we can consider to save data and retrieve it when needed. It is faster than the database operation. In ASP.NET Core, we can use in-memory caching that stores the data in the memory of the server, but for a web farm or a load balancing scenario where an application is deployed to multiple places, it is recommended to use a distributed cache. Microsoft Azure also provides a Redis cache which is a distributed cache that exposes an endpoint that can be used to store values on the cloud and can be retrieved when they are needed.

To use the in-memory cache in the ASP.NET Core project, we can simply add the memory cache in the ConfigureServices method, which is shown as follows:

```
public void ConfigureServices(IServiceCollection services)
{
  services.AddMvc();
  services.AddMemoryCache();
}
```

Then, we can inject IMemoryCache in our controllers or page models through dependency injection and set or get values using the Set and Get methods.

Data structures

Choosing the right data structure plays a vital role in application performance. Before choosing any data structure, it is highly recommended to think about whether it is an overhead or it literally solves a particular use case. Some key factors to be considered while choosing an appropriate data structure are as follows:

- Know about the type of data you need to store
- Know how the data grows and whether there is any drawback when it grows
- Know if you need to access your data through an index or key/value pairs and choose the appropriate data structure
- Know if you need synchronized access and choose thread-safe collections

There are many other factors when choosing the right data structure, and they have already been covered in `Chapter 4`, *Data Structures and Writing Optimized Code in C#*.

Communication

Nowadays, communication has become an important epitome in any application, and the primary factor is the rapid evolution of technology. Applications such as web-based applications, mobile applications, IoT applications, and other distributed applications perform different types of communication over the wire. We can take an example of an application that has a web frontend deployed on some cloud instance, invoking some service deployed on a separate instance in the cloud and performing some backend connectivity to the database which is hosted locally. Besides this, we can have an IoT application that sends the room temperature by calling some service over the internet, and many more. Certain factors that need to be considered when designing distributed application are as follows:

Using lighter interfaces

Avoid multiple round trips to the server that adds more network latency and decreases application performance. Using the unit of work pattern avoids sending redundant operations to the server and performs one single operation to communicate to the backend service. The unit of work groups all the messages as a single unit and processes them as one unit.

Minimizing message size

Use as little data as possible to communicate to the service. For example, there is a Person API that provides some GET, POST, PUT, and DELETE methods to perform a CRUD operation on that backend database. To delete a person's record, we can just pass the ID (primary key) of the person as a parameter to the service rather than passing the whole object as a parameter. Moreover, use objects that are less bloated with properties or methods that offer a minimal set of artifacts. The best case is to use **POCO** (**Plain Old CLR object**) entities that have minimal dependencies on other objects which contain only those properties that are necessary to be sent across the wire.

Queuing communication

For larger object or complex operation, decoupling the single request/response channel from the distributed messaging channel increases the application's performance. For large, chunky operations, we can design and distribute communication into multiple components. For example, there is a website that calls a service to upload an image, and, once it is uploaded, it does some processing to extract a thumbnail and saves it in the database. One way is to do both uploading and processing in a single call, but at times when the user uploads a larger image or if the image processing takes a longer time, the user may face a request timeout exception, and the request will terminate.

With the queuing architecture, we can distribute these two operations into separate calls. The user uploads the image which is saved in the filesystem, and the image path will be saved into storage. A service running in the background will pick up that file and do the processing asynchronously. Meanwhile, when the backend service is processing, the control is returned to the user, where the user can see some in-progress notification. Finally, when the thumbnail is generated, the user will be notified:

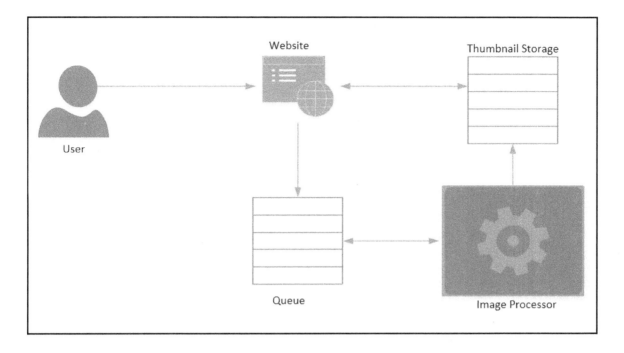

Resource management

Every server has a limited set of resources. No matter how good the server specification, if the application is not designed to utilize resources in an efficient manner, this leads to performance issues. There are certain best practices that need to be addressed to optimally use server resources when designing .NET Core applications.

Avoiding improper use of threads

Creating a new thread for each task without monitoring or aborting the lifecycle of the thread is a bad practice. Threads are good to perform multitasking and to utilize multiple resources of the server to run things in parallel. However, if the design is to create threads for each request, this can slow down the application's performance, as the CPU will take more time in the context of switching between the threads rather than executing the actual job.

Whenever we use threads, we should always try to keep a shared thread pool where any new item that needs to be executed waits in the queue if the thread is busy, and is acquired when it is available. This way, thread management is easy and server resources will be used efficiently.

Disposing objects in a timely fashion

CLR (**Common Language Runtime**) provides automatic memory management, and the objects instantiated with a new keyword do not require to be garbage collected explicitly; **GC** (**Garbage Collection**) does the job. However, non-managed resources are not automatically released by the GC and should be explicitly collected by implementing the IDisposable interface. Such resources could be database connections, file handlers, sockets, and so on. To learn more about disposing of unmanaged resources in .NET Core, please refer to Chapter 6, *Memory Management Techniques in .NET Core.*

Acquiring resources when they are required

Always acquire resources only when they are required. Instantiating objects ahead of time is not a good practice. It takes unnecessary memory and utilizes resources of the system. Furthermore, use *try, catch,* and *finally* to block and release objects in the *finally* block. This way, if any exception occurs, the objects which have been instantiated within the method will be released.

Concurrency

In concurrent programming, many objects may access the same resource at the same time, and keeping them thread-safe is the primary objective. In .NET Core, we can use locks to provide synchronized access. However, there are cases where a thread has to wait for a longer time to get access to resources, and this makes applications unresponsive.

The best practice is to apply for synchronized access only for those specific lines of code where the actual resource needs to be thread-safe, for example, where the locks can be used, which are the database operations, file handling, bank account access, and many other critical sections in the application. These need synchronized access so that they can be handled one thread at a time.

Summary

Writing cleaner code, following the architecture and design principles, and adhering to the best practices play a significant role in application performance. If the code if baggy and repetitive, it can increase the chances of errors, increase complexity, and affect performance.

In this chapter, we have learned some coding principles that make the application code look cleaner and easier to understand. If the code is clean, it offers other developers a way to understand it completely and helps in many other ways. Later on, we learned some basic design principles that are considered to be the core principles when designing applications. Principles such as KISS, YAGNI, DRY, Separation of Concerns, and SOLID are highly essential in software design, and caching and choosing the right data structure have a significant impact on performance and increase performance if they are used properly. Finally, we learned some best practices that should be considered when handling communication, resource management, and concurrency.

The next chapter is a detailed introduction to memory management, where we will explore some techniques of memory management in .NET Core.

6
Memory Management Techniques in .NET Core

Memory management significantly affects the performance of any application. When the application is run, .NET CLR (Common Language Runtime) allocates many objects in memory, and they stay there until they are not needed, until new objects are created and are allocated space, or until the GC runs (as it does occasionally) to release unused objects and make more space available for other objects. Most of the job is done by the GC itself, which runs intelligently and frees up space for the objects by removing those that are not needed. However, there are certain practices that can help any application to avoid performance issues and run smoothly.

In Chapter 2, *Understanding .NET Core Internals and Measuring Performance*, we already learned about how garbage collection works and how generations are maintained in .NET. In this chapter, we will focus on some recommended best practices and patterns that avoid memory leakage and make the application performant.

The following are the topics that we will learn:

- Memory allocation process overview
- Analysing memory through SOS debugging
- Memory fragmentation
- Avoiding finalizers
- Best practices to dispose of objects in .NET Core

Memory allocation process overview

Memory allocation is the process of allocating objects in memory when the application is running. It is done by the **Common Language Runtime** (**CLR**). When the object is initialized (using a `new` keyword), the GC checks whether the generation reaches the threshold and performs garbage collection. This means that when the system memory reaches its limit, the GC is invoked. When an application runs, the GC register itself receives an event notification about the system memory, and when the system reaches its particular limit, it invokes garbage collection.

On the other hand, we can also programmatically invoke the GC using the `GC.Collect` method. However, as the GC is a highly fine-tuned algorithm and automatically behaves as per memory allocation patterns, calling it explicitly can affect performance, and so it is strongly recommended that you don't use it in production.

Analysing CLR internals through the SOS debugger in .NET Core

SOS is a debugging extension that is shipped with Windows and is available for Linux as well. It helps to debug .NET Core applications by providing information about CLR internals, especially memory allocation, the number of objects created, and other details about the CLR. We can use the SOS extension in .NET Core to debug the native machine code, which is specific to each platform.

 To install the SOS extension for Windows, install the **Windows Driver Kit** (**WDK**) from
https://developer.microsoft.com/en-us/windows/hardware/download-kits-windows-hardware-development.

When the Windows Driver Kit is installed, we can use various commands to analyze the CLR internals about the application and identify which objects are taking up the most memory in the heap and optimize them accordingly.

As we know that, in .NET Core, there is no executable file generated, we can use *dotnet cli* commands to execute the .NET Core application. The commands to run the .NET Core application are as follows:

- `dotnet run`
- `dotnet applicationpath/applicationname.dll`

We can run either of the preceding commands to run the .NET Core application. In the case of the ASP.NET Core application, we can go to the root of the application folder, where `Views`, `wwwroot`, `Models`, `Controllers` and other files reside, and run the following command:

```
Directory of D:\Authoring\C#7.0NetCore2.0\My Chapters\Chapter6\Chapter6\Chapter6WebApp

24-Dec-2017  09:55 PM    <DIR>          .
24-Dec-2017  09:55 PM    <DIR>          ..
24-Dec-2017  09:55 PM                36 .bowerrc
24-Dec-2017  09:55 PM               178 appsettings.Development.json
24-Dec-2017  09:55 PM               113 appsettings.json
24-Dec-2017  09:55 PM    <DIR>          bin
24-Dec-2017  09:55 PM               207 bower.json
24-Dec-2017  09:55 PM               628 bundleconfig.json
24-Dec-2017  09:55 PM               397 Chapter6WebApp.csproj
24-Dec-2017  09:55 PM    <DIR>          Controllers
24-Dec-2017  09:55 PM    <DIR>          Models
24-Dec-2017  11:12 PM    <DIR>          obj
24-Dec-2017  09:55 PM               631 Program.cs
24-Dec-2017  09:55 PM    <DIR>          Properties
24-Dec-2017  09:55 PM             1,472 Startup.cs
24-Dec-2017  09:55 PM    <DIR>          Views
24-Dec-2017  09:55 PM    <DIR>          wwwroot
               8 File(s)          3,662 bytes
               9 Dir(s)  41,166,479,360 bytes free
```

On the other hand, debugging tools usually require the `.exe` file or the process ID to dump information related to the CLR internals. To run the SOS debugger, we can go to the path where the Windows Driver Kit is installed (the directory path will be `{driveletter}:Program Files (x86)Windows Kits10Debuggersx64`) and run the following command:

```
windbg dotnet {application path}
```

Here is a screenshot that shows you how to run the ASP.NET Core application using the `windbg` command:

```
C:\Program Files (x86)\Windows Kits\10\Debuggers\x64>windbg dotnet D:\Authoring\C#7.0NetCore2.0\My Chapters\Chapter6
\Chapter6\Chapter6WebApp\bin\debug\netcoreapp2.0\chapter6webapp.dll
```

Once you run the preceding command, it will open up the Windbg window and the debugger, as follows:

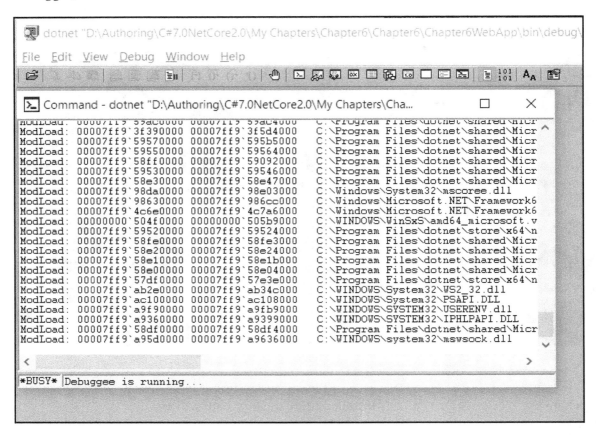

You can stop the debugger by clicking **Debug** | **Break** and running the sos command to load the information about .NET Core CLR.

Execute the following command from the Windbg window and hit *Enter*:

```
.loadby sos coreclr
```

The following screenshot is of the interface from which you can type and run the preceding command:

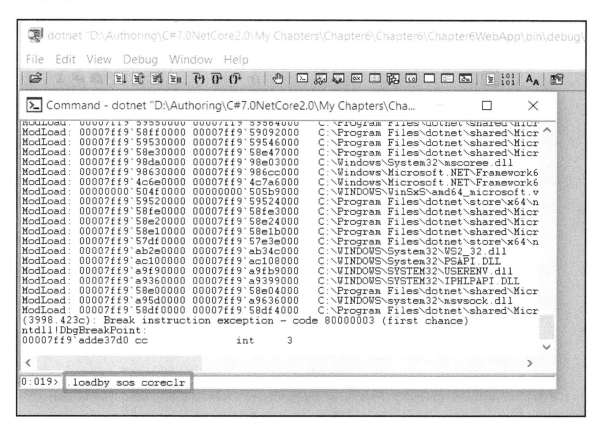

Finally, we can run the `!DumpHeap` command to see the complete statistical details of the objects heap:

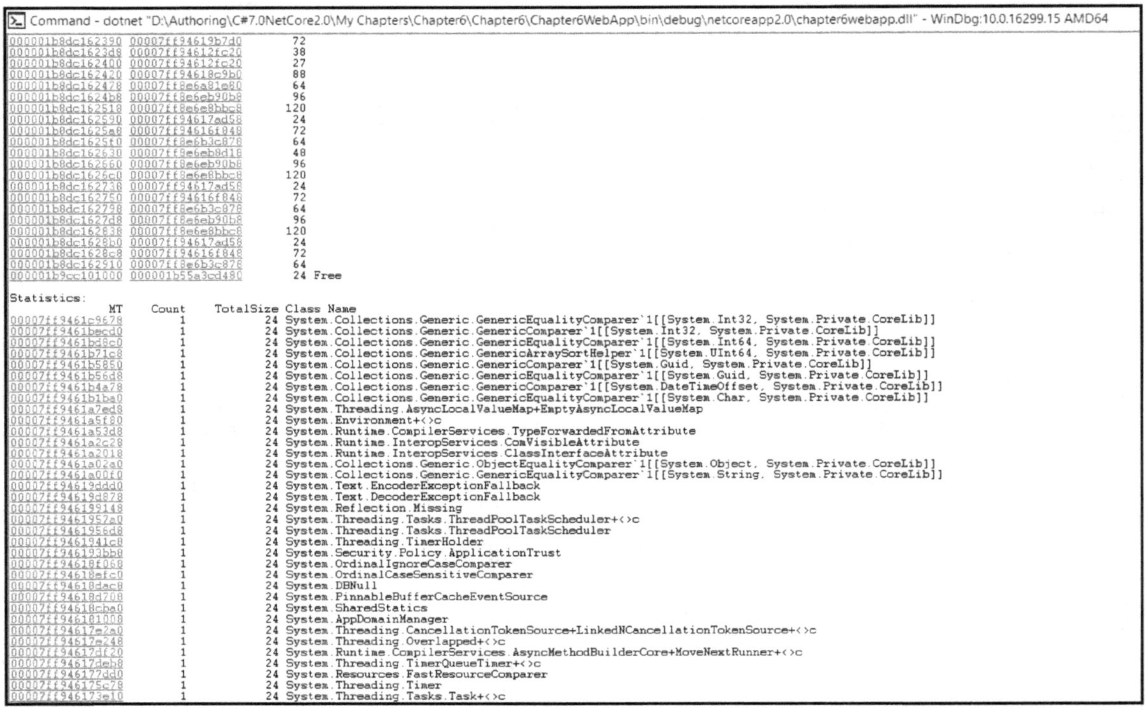

In the preceding screenshot, the first three columns as shown in the following screenshot, represent the `Address`, `Method` table and `Size` of each method:

Using the preceding information, it provides the statistics that classify the objects stored on the heap by their type. `MT` is the method table of that type, `Count` is the total number of instances of that type, `TotalSize` is the total memory size occupied by all the instances of that type, and `Classname` represents the actual type that takes up that space on the heap.

There are a few more commands that we can use to get specific details, listed as follows:

Switch	Command	Description
Statistics	`!DumpHeap -stat`	Shows only statistical details
Type	`!DumpHeap -type TypeName`	Shows the statistics for a particular type stored on the heap
Finalization queue	`!FinalizationQueue`	Show details about the finalizers

This tool helps developers to investigate how objects are allocated on the heap. In a practical scenario, we can run our application on a test or staging server by running this tool in the background and examining the detailed statistics about the objects stored on the heap for a particular point of time.

Memory fragmentation

Memory fragmentation is one of the primary causes of performance issues in .NET applications. When the object is instantiated, it occupies space in the memory, and when it is not needed, it is garbage collected, and that allocated memory block becomes available. This occurs when the object is allocated a larger space with respect to the size available in that memory segment/block and waits until space becomes available. Memory fragmentation is a problem that occurs when most of the memory is allocated in a larger number of non-contiguous blocks. When a larger size of object stores or occupies the larger memory block and the memory only contains smaller chunks of free blocks that are available, this causes fragmentation, and the system fails to allocate that object in memory.

.NET maintains two types of heap—namely the **small object heap (SOH)** and **large object heap (LOH)**. Objects that are greater than 85,000 bytes are stored in LOH. The key difference between SOH and LOH is that in LOH there is no compaction being done by the GC. Compaction is the process that is done at the time of garbage collection, where objects stored in the SOH are moved to eliminate the smaller chunks of free space available and increase the total space available as one form of large memory chunk that can be used by other objects, which reduces fragmentation. However, in LOH, there is no compaction being done by the GC implicitly. Objects that are large in size are stored in LOH and create fragmentation issues. Moreover, if we compare LOH with SOH, the compaction cost for LOH is moderately high and involves significant overhead, where the GC needs twice as much memory space to move objects for defragmentation. This is another reason why LOH is not defragmented implicitly by the GC.

The following is a representation of memory fragmentation, where the white blocks represent the unallocated memory space, and are followed by an allocated block:

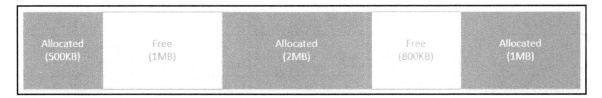

Suppose an object that has a size of 1.5 MB wants to be allocated some memory. It will not find any free space available, even though the total amount of memory available is 1.8 MB. The reason for this is memory fragmentation:

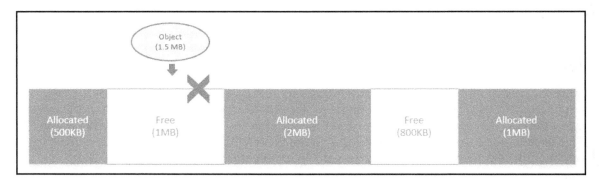

On the other hand, if the memory is defragmented, the object can easily use the space that is available and will be allocated:

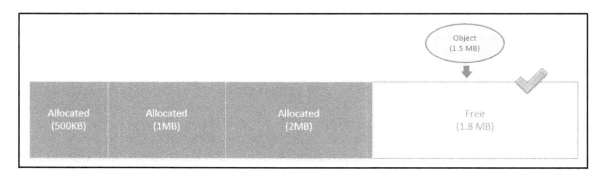

In .NET Core, we can perform compaction in LOH explicitly using `GCSettings`, as follows:

```
GCSettings.LargeObjectHeapCompactionMode =
GCLargeObjectHeapCompactionMode.CompactOnce;
GC.Collect();
```

Avoiding finalizers

Using finalizers is not a good practice to use in .NET Core applications. Objects that use finalizers stay in memory longer and ultimately affect the application's performance.

Objects that are not required by the application at a particular point in time stay in the memory so that their `Finalizer` method can be called. For example, if the object is considered dead by the GC in generation 0, it will always survive in generation 1.

In .NET Core, CLR maintains a separate thread to run the `Finalizer` method. All the objects that contain the `Finalizer` method are placed into the finalization queue. Any object that is no longer required by the application is placed in the F-Reachable queue, which is then executed by the dedicated finalizer thread.

The following diagram shows an `object1` object that contains a `Finalizer` method. The `Finalizer` method is placed in the finalization queue and the object occupies the memory space in the **Gen0** (generation 0) heap:

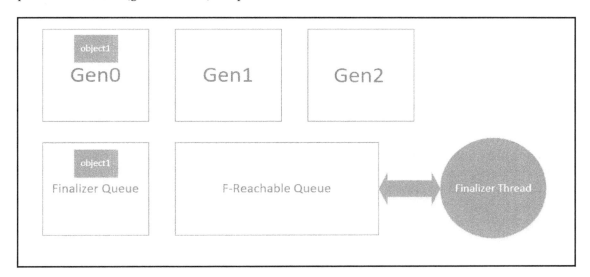

When the object is no longer required, it will be moved from **Gen0** (generation 0) to **Gen1** (generation 1) and from the **Finalizer Queue** to the **F-Reachable Queue**:

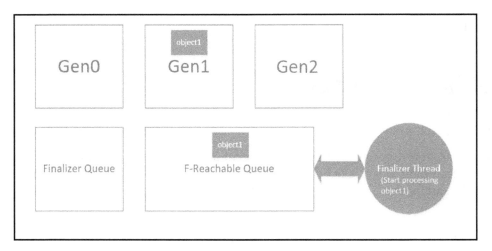

Once the finalizer thread runs the method in the **F-Reachable Queue**, it will be removed from the memory by the GC.

In .NET Core, the finalizer can be defined as follows:

```
public class FileLogger
{
  //Finalizer implementation
   ~FileLogger()
  {
    //dispose objects
  }
}
```

Usually, this method is used to dispose of unmanaged objects and contains some code. However, a code can contain bugs that affect performance. For example, we have three objects that are queued in a finalization queue, which then waits for the first object to be released by the finalizer thread so they can be processed. Now, suppose that a bug in the first `Finalizer` method causes a problem and delays the finalizer thread in returning and processing the rest of the methods. After some time, more objects will come into the finalization queue and wait for the finalizer thread to process, impacting the applications, performance.

The best practice to dispose of objects is to use the IDisposable interface rather than implementing the Finalizer method. If you are using the Finalizer method for some reason, it is always good to implement the IDisposable interface as well and suppress finalization by calling the GC.SuppressFinalize method.

Best practices for disposing of objects in .NET Core

We have learned in the previous section that object disposal in .NET Core is automatically done by the GC. Nevertheless, disposing of objects in your code is always a good practice, and is highly recommended when you are working with unmanaged objects. In this section, we will explore some best practices that can be used to dispose of objects while writing code in .NET Core.

Introduction to the IDisposable interface

IDisposable is a simple interface that contains one Dispose method, takes no parameter, and returns void:

```
public interface IDisposable
{
  void Dispose();
}
```

It is used to release unmanaged resources. So if any class implements the IDisposable interface, it means that the class contains unmanaged resources and these have to be released by calling the Dispose method of the class.

What are unmanaged resources?

Any resource that is outside of your application boundary is considered an unmanaged resource. It could be a database, filesystem, web service, or a similar resource. To access the database, we use the managed .NET API to open or close the connection and execute various commands. However, the actual connection to the database is not managed. The same is true for the filesystem and web services where we use managed .NET APIs to interact with them, but they use unmanaged resources in the backend that are not managed. The IDisposable interface is the best fit for all such scenarios.

Using IDisposable

Here is a simple DataManager class that uses a System.Data.SQL API to perform database operations on an SQL server database:

```
public class DataManager : IDisposable
{
  private SqlConnection _connection;
  //Returns the list of users from database
  public DataTable GetUsers()
  {
    //Invoke OpenConnection to instantiate the _connection object

    OpenConnection();

    //Executing command in a using block to dispose command object
    using(var command =new SqlCommand())
    {
      command.Connection = _connection;
      command.CommandText = "Select * from Users";

      //Executing reader in a using block to dispose reader object
      using (var reader = command.ExecuteReader())
      {
        var dt = new DataTable();
        dt.Load(reader);
        return dt;
      }

    }
  }
  private void OpenConnection()
  {
    if (_connection == null)
```

```
    {
        _connection = new SqlConnection(@"Integrated Security=SSPI;
        Persist Security Info=False;Initial Catalog=SampleDB;
        Data Source=.sqlexpress");
        _connection.Open();
    }
}

//Disposing _connection object
public void Dispose() {
    Console.WriteLine("Disposing object");
    _connection.Close();
    _connection.Dispose();
}
}
```

In the preceding code, we have implemented the IDisposable interface which, in turn, implemented the Dispose method to clean up the SQL connection object. We have also called the connection's Dispose method, which will chain up the process in the pipeline and close the underlying objects.

From the calling program, we can use the using block to instantiate the DatabaseManager object that invokes the Dispose method after calling the GetUsers method:

```
static void Main(string[] args)
{
    using(DataManager manager=new DataManager())
    {
        manager.GetUsers();
    }
}
```

The using block is a C# construct that is rendered by the compiler in a try finally block and calls the Dispose method in the finally block. So this means that when you are using a using block, we don't have to call the Dispose method explicitly. Alternatively, the preceding code can be written in the following way as well, and this particular code format is internally managed by the using block:

```
static void Main(string[] args)
{
    DataManager _manager;
    try
    {
        _manager = new DataManager();
    }
    finally
```

```
  {
    _manager.Dispose();
  }
}
```

When to implement the IDisposable interface

We already know that the IDisposable interface should be used whenever we need to release unmanaged resources. However, there is a standard rule that should be considered when dealing with the disposal of objects. The rule states that if the instance within the class implements the IDisposable interface, we should implement IDisposable on the consuming class as well. For example, the preceding class DatabaseManager class uses SqlConnection, where SqlConnection implements the IDisposable interface internally. To address this rule, we will implement the IDisposable interface and invoke the instance's Dispose method.

Here is a better example that invokes the protected Dispose method from the DatabaseManager Dispose method and passes a Boolean value indicating that the object is being disposed of. Ultimately, we will call the GC.SuppressFinalize method that tells the GC that the object is already cleaned up, preventing a redundant garbage collection from being called:

```
public void Dispose() {
  Console.WriteLine("Disposing object");
  Dispose(true);
  GC.SuppressFinalize(this);
}
protected virtual void Dispose(Boolean disposing)
{
  if (disposing)
  {
    if (_connection != null)
    {
      _connection.Close();
      _connection.Dispose();
      //set _connection to null, so next time it won't hit this block
      _connection = null;
    }
  }
}
}
```

The reason we have kept the parameterized `Dispose` method `protected` and `virtual` is so that the child classes if derived from the `DatabaseManager` class can override the `Dispose` method and clean up their own resources. This ensures that each class in the object tree will clean up its resources. Child classes dispose of their resources and call `Dispose` on the base class, and so on.

Finalizer and Dispose

The `Finalizer` method is called by the GC, whereas the `Dispose` method has to be called by the developer explicitly in the program. The GC doesn't know if the class contains a `Dispose` method, and it needs to be called when the object is disposing to clean up the unmanaged resources. In this scenario, where we need to strictly clean up the resources rather than relying on the caller to call the `Dispose` method of the object, we should implement the `Finalizer` method.

The following is a modified example of the `DatabaseManager` class that implements the `Finalizer` method:

```
public class DataManager : IDisposable
{
  private SqlConnection _connection;
  //Returns the list of users from database
  public DataTable GetUsers()
  {
    //Invoke OpenConnection to instantiate the _connection object

    OpenConnection();

    //Executing command in a using block to dispose command object
    using(var command =new SqlCommand())
    {
      command.Connection = _connection;
      command.CommandText = "Select * from Users";

      //Executing reader in a using block to dispose reader object
      using (var reader = command.ExecuteReader())
      {
        var dt = new DataTable();
        dt.Load(reader);
        return dt;
      }
    }
  }
  private void OpenConnection()
```

```
{
  if (_conn == null)
  {
    _connection = new SqlConnection(@"Integrated Security=SSPI;
    Persist Security Info=False;Initial Catalog=SampleDB;
    Data Source=.sqlexpress");
    _connection.Open();
  }
}

//Disposing _connection object
public void Dispose() {
  Console.WriteLine("Disposing object");
  Dispose(true);
  GC.SuppressFinalize(this);
}

private void Dispose(Boolean disposing)
{
  if(disposing) {
    //clean up any managed resources, if called from the
    //finalizer, all the managed resources will already
    //be collected by the GC
  }
  if (_connection != null)
  {
    _connection.Close();
    _connection.Dispose();
    //set _connection to null, so next time it won't hit this block
    _connection = null;
  }

}
//Implementing Finalizer
~DataManager(){
  Dispose(false);
}
}
```

In the preceding code snippet, we have modified the `Dispose` method and added the finalizer using a destructor syntax, `~DataManager`. When the GC runs, the finalizer is invoked and calls the `Dispose` method by passing a false flag as a Boolean parameter. In the `Dispose` method, we will clean up the `connection` object. During the finalization stage, the managed resources will already be cleaned up by the GC, so the `Dispose` method will now only clean up the unmanaged resources from the finalizer. However, a developer can explicitly dispose of objects by calling the `Dispose` method and passing a true flag as a Boolean parameter to clean up managed resources.

Summary

This chapter was focused on memory management. We learned some best practices and the actual underlying process of how memory management is done in .NET. We explored the debugging tool, which can be used by developers to investigate an object's memory allocation on the heap. We also learned about memory fragmentation, finalizers, and how to implement a dispose pattern to clean up resources by implementing the `IDisposable` interface.

In the next chapter, we will be creating an application following a microservices architecture. A microservice architecture is a highly performant and scalable architecture that helps the application to scale out easily. The following chapter provides you with a complete understanding of how an application can be developed following the best practices and principles.

7
Securing and Implementing Resilience in .NET Core Applications

Security and resilience are two important aspects that should be considered when developing applications of any scale. Security protects an application's secrets, performs authentication, and provides authorized access to secure content, whereas resiliency embraces the application if it fails so that it can degrade gracefully. Resiliency makes an application highly available and allows the application to function properly at the time when an error occurs or when it is in a faulty state. It is widely used with the microservices architecture, where an application is decomposed into multiple services and each service communicates with other services to perform an operation.

There are various techniques and libraries available in .NET Core that we can use to implement security and resiliency. In ASP.NET Core applications, we can use Identity to implement user authentication/authorization, a popular Polly framework to implement patterns such as circuit breaker, the retry pattern, and others.

In this chapter, we will look at the following topics:

- Introduction to resilient applications
- Implementing health checks to monitor application performance
- Implementing the retry pattern in ASP.NET Core applications to retry operations on transient faults
- Implementing circuit breaker patterns to prevent calls that are likely to fail
- Protecting ASP.NET Core applications and enabling authentication and authorization using the Identity framework
- Using safe storage to store application secrets

Introduction to resilient applications

Developing applications with resiliency as an important factor always makes your customers happy. Today, applications are distributed by nature and involve lots of communication over the wire. Problems arise when the service is down or not responding on time due to network failure, which eventually leads to a delay before the client operation is terminated. The purpose of resiliency is to make your application recover from a failure and make it responsive again.

Complexity increases when you call one service and that service calls another service, and so on. In a long chain of operations, considering resiliency is important. This is the reason it is one of the most widely adopted principles in microservice architecture.

Resilient policies

Resilient policies are classified into two categories:

- Reactive policies
- Proactive policies

In this chapter, we will implement both reactive and proactive policies using the Polly framework, which can be used with .NET Core applications.

Reactive policies

According to the reactive policy, we should instantly retry the service request if the request fails on its first attempt. To implement the reactive policy, we can use the following patterns:

- **Retry**: Retries immediately when the request fails
- **Circuit breaker**: Stops all requests to a service in a faulted state
- **Fallback**: Returns a default response if the service is in a faulted state

Implementing the retry pattern

The retry pattern is used to retry the faulted service a number of times in order to get a response. It is widely used in scenarios involving intercommunication between services, where one service is dependent on another service to perform a particular operation. Transient faults occur when services are hosted separately and communicate over the wire, most likely over a HTTP protocol.

The following diagram represents two services: a user registration service that registers and save the user's record in a database, and an email service to send a confirmation email to the user so that they can activate their account. Suppose an email service does not respond. This will return some sort of error, and if a retry pattern is implemented, it will retry the request the number of times it has been implemented to do so, and will call the email service if it fails:

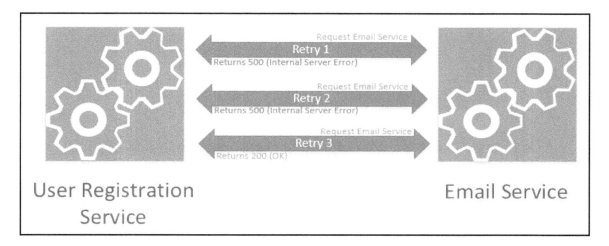

The **User Registration Service** and the **Email Service** are ASP.NET Core Web API projects where user registration implements the retry pattern. We will use the Polly framework by adding it as a NuGet package in the user registration service. To add Polly, we can execute the following command from the NuGet package manager console window in Visual Studio:

```
Install-Package Polly
```

The Polly framework is based on policies. You can define policies that contain specific configurations related to the pattern you are implementing and then invoke that policy by calling its ExecuteAsync method.

Here is the `UserController` which contains a POST method that implements a retry pattern to invoke the email service:

```
[Route("api/[controller]")]
public class UserController : Controller
{

  HttpClient _client;
  public UserController(HttpClient client)
  {
    _client = client;
  }
  // POST api/values
  [HttpPost]
  public void Post([FromBody]User user)
  {
    //Email service URL
    string emailService = "http://localhost:80/api/Email";

    //Serialize user object into JSON string
    HttpContent content = new
StringContent(JsonConvert.SerializeObject(user));

    //Setting Content-Type to application/json
    _client.DefaultRequestHeaders
    .Accept
    .Add(new MediaTypeWithQualityHeaderValue("application/json"));


    int maxRetries = 3;

    //Define Retry policy and set max retries limit and duration between
each retry to 3 seconds
    var retryPolicy =
Policy.Handle<HttpRequestException>().WaitAndRetryAsync(
    maxRetries, sleepDuration=> TimeSpan.FromSeconds(3));


    //Call service and wrap HttpClient PostAsync into retry policy
    retryPolicy.ExecuteAsync(async () => {
      var response = _client.PostAsync(emailService, content).Result;
      response.EnsureSuccessStatusCode();
    });
  }
}
```

In the preceding code, we have used the `HttpClient` class to make a RESTful request to the email service API. The `HTTP POST` method receives a user object that contains the following five properties:

```
public class User
{
  public string FirstName { get; set; }
  public string LastName { get; set; }
  public string EmailAddress { get; set; }
  public string UserName { get; set; }
  public string Password { get; set; }
}
```

Since the request will be sent in JSON format, we have to set the `Content-Type` header value to `application/json`. Then, we have to define the retry policy to wait and retry the operation every three seconds, with the maximum amount of retries being three. Finally, we call the `ExecuteAsync` method to invoke the `client.PostAsync` method so that it calls the email service.

After running the preceding example, if the email service is down or throws an exception, it will be retried three times to try and get the required response.

Implementing circuit breaker

Implementing the retry pattern is a good practice when calling services that are communicating over a network. However, the calling mechanism itself takes resources and bandwidth to execute the operation and delay the response. If the services are already in a faulted state, it is not always a good practice to retry it multiple times for every request. This is where circuit breaker plays its role.

Circuit breaker works in three states, as shown in the following diagram:

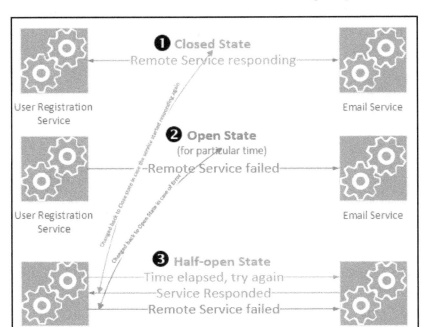

Initially, the circuit breaker is in a **Closed State**, which means the communication between services are working and the target remote service is responding. If the target remote service fails, the circuit breaker changes to **Open State**. When the state becomes open, then all subsequent requests cannot invoke the target remote service for a particular, specified time, and directly returns the response to the caller. Once the time elapses, the circuit turns to **Half-open State** and tries to invoke the target remote service to get the response. If the response is received successfully, the circuit breaker changes back to **Closed State**, or if it fails, the state changes back to closed and remains closed for the time specified in the configuration.

To implement the circuit breaker pattern, we will use the same Polly framework, which you can add from the NuGet package. We can add the circuit breaker policy as follows:

```
var circuitBreakerPolicy = Policy.HandleResult<HttpResponseMessage>(result
=> !result.IsSuccessStatusCode)
   .CircuitBreakerAsync(3, TimeSpan.FromSeconds(10), OnBreak, OnReset,
OnHalfOpen);
```

Add the preceding circuit breaker policy inside the ConfigureServices method in the Startup class. The reason for defining it in the Startup class is to inject the circuit breaker object as a singleton object through **Dependency Injection** (**DI**). Therefore, all requests will share the same instance and the state will be maintained properly.

While defining the circuit breaker policy, we set the number of events allowed before breaking the circuit as three, which checks how many times the request has failed and breaks the circuit once it reaches the threshold value of three. It will keep the circuit break *Open* for 10 seconds and then change the state to *Half-Open* when the first request comes in after the time has elapsed.

Finally, if the remote service is still failing ,the circuit state changes to the *Open* state again; otherwise, it is set as *Close*. We have also defined OnBreak, OnReset, and OnHalfOpen delegates that are invoked when the circuit state changes. We can log this information somewhere in the database or file system if required. Add these delegate methods in the Startup class:

```
private void OnBreak(DelegateResult<HttpResponseMessage> responseMessage,
TimeSpan timeSpan)
{
   //Log to file system
}
private void OnReset()
{
   //log to file system
}
private void OnHalfOpen()
{
   // log to file system
}
```

Now, we will add the circuitBreakerPolicy and HttpClient objects using DI in the ConfigureServices method in the Startup class:

```
services.AddSingleton<HttpClient>();
services.AddSingleton<CircuitBreakerPolicy<HttpResponseMessage>>(circuitBre
akerPolgicy);
```

Here is our `UserController` that takes the `HttpClient` and `CircuitBreakerPolicy` object in the parameterized constructor:

```
public class UserController : Controller
{
  HttpClient _client;
  CircuitBreakerPolicy<HttpResponseMessage> _circuitBreakerPolicy;
  public UserController(HttpClient client,
  CircuitBreakerPolicy<HttpResponseMessage> circuitBreakerPolicy)
  {
    _client = client;
    _circuitBreakerPolicy = circuitBreakerPolicy;
  }
}
```

And this is the `HTTP POST` method that uses the circuit breaker policy and invokes the email service:

```
// POST api/values
[HttpPost]
public async Task<IActionResult> Post([FromBody]User user)
{

  //Email service URL
  string emailService = "http://localhost:80/api/Email";

  //Serialize user object into JSON string
  HttpContent content = new
StringContent(JsonConvert.SerializeObject(user));

  //Setting Content-Type to application/json
  _client.DefaultRequestHeaders
  .Accept
  .Add(new MediaTypeWithQualityHeaderValue("application/json"));

  //Execute operation using circuit breaker
  HttpResponseMessage response = await
_circuitBreakerPolicy.ExecuteAsync(() =>
  _client.PostAsync(emailService, content));

  //Check if response status code is success
  if (response.IsSuccessStatusCode)
  {
    var result = response.Content.ReadAsStringAsync();
    return Ok(result);
  }
```

```
//If the response status is not success, it returns the actual state
//followed with the response content
return StatusCode((int)response.StatusCode,
response.Content.ReadAsStringAsync());
}
```

This is the classic circuit breaker example. Polly also comes with an advanced circuit breaker, which is more useful in cases where you have to break the circuit based on the percentage of failed requests in a particular amount of time. When working with big applications or applications that involve lots of transactions within a minute, there's a chance that 2% to 5% of transactions will fail due to other non-transient failure issues, so we don't want the circuit to break. In this case, we can implement the advanced circuit breaker pattern and define the policy in our `ConfigureServices` method, which is shown as follows:

```
public void ConfigureServices(IServiceCollection services)
{
  var circuitBreakerPolicy = Policy.HandleResult<HttpResponseMessage>(
  result => !result.IsSuccessStatusCode)
  .AdvancedCircuitBreaker(0.1, TimeSpan.FromSeconds(60),5,
TimeSpan.FromSeconds(10),
  OnBreak, OnReset, OnHalfOpen);
  services.AddSingleton<HttpClient>();
services.AddSingleton<CircuitBreakerPolicy<HttpResponseMessage>>(circuitBre
akerPolicy);
}
```

The first parameter in the `AdvancedCircuitBreakerAsync` method contains a value of 0.1, which is the percentage of requests that have failed in the time frame, which is 60 seconds, as specified in the second parameter. The third parameter which, defines the value of 5, is the minimum throughput of requests being served in that particular time, as specified in the second parameter which is 60 seconds. Finally, the fourth parameter defines the amount of time the circuit remains open if any request fails and tries to serve the request again once the time has elapsed. The Other parameters are just delegate methods that are called when each state is changed, which is the same as in the previous classic circuit breaker example.

Wrapping the circuit breaker with retry

So far, we have learned how circuit breaker and retry patterns can be used and implemented using the Polly framework. The retry pattern is used to retry the request if it fails for a specified amount of time, where circuit breaker keeps the state of the circuit and, based on the threshold of the requests being failed, makes the circuit open and stops calling the remote service for some time, as specified in the configuration to save network bandwidth.

With the Polly framework, we can use the retry and circuit breaker patterns in conjunction and wrap the circuit breaker with the retry pattern to open the circuit if the retry pattern reaches the count of the failed request threshold limit.

In this section, we will develop a custom `HttpClient` class that provides methods such as GET, POST, PUT, and DELETE, and use retry and circuit breaker policies to make it resilient.

Create a new `IResilientHttpClient` interface and add four methods for HTTP GET, POST, PUT, and DELETE:

```
public interface IResilientHttpClient
{
   HttpResponseMessage Get(string uri);

   HttpResponseMessage Post<T>(string uri, T item);

   HttpResponseMessage Delete(string uri);

   HttpResponseMessage Put<T>(string uri, T item);
}
```

Now, create a new class called `ResilientHttpClient`, which implements the `IResilientHttpClient` interface. We will add a parameterized constructor to inject the circuit breaker policy and a `HttpClient` object, which will be used to make HTTP GET, POST, PUT, and DELETE requests. Here is the constructor implementation of the `ResilientHttpClient` class:

```
public class ResilientHttpClient : IResilientHttpClient
{
   static CircuitBreakerPolicy<HttpResponseMessage> _circuitBreakerPolicy;
   static Policy<HttpResponseMessage> _retryPolicy;
   HttpClient _client;
   public ResilientHttpClient(HttpClient client,
   CircuitBreakerPolicy<HttpResponseMessage> circuitBreakerPolicy)
   {
     _client = client;
```

```
_client.DefaultRequestHeaders.Accept.Clear();
_client.DefaultRequestHeaders.Accept.Add(
new MediaTypeWithQualityHeaderValue("application/json"));

//circuit breaker policy injected as defined in the Startup class
_circuitBreakerPolicy = circuitBreakerPolicy;

//Defining retry policy
_retryPolicy = Policy.HandleResult<HttpResponseMessage>(x =>
{
    var result = !x.IsSuccessStatusCode;
    return result;
})
//Retry 3 times and for each retry wait for 3 seconds
.WaitAndRetry(3, sleepDuration => TimeSpan.FromSeconds(3));

    }
}
```

In the preceding code, we have defined the
`CircuitBreakerPolicy<HttpResponseMessage>` and `HttpClient` objects, which are
injected through DI. We have defined the retry policy and set the retry threshold to three
times, where each retry will wait for three seconds before making a call to the service.

Next, we will create the `ExecuteWithRetryandCircuitBreaker` method, which takes a
URI and a delegate function that will be executed within the retry and circuit breaker
policies. Here is the code snippet of the `ExecuteWithRetryandCircuitBreaker` method:

```
//Wrap function body in Retry and Circuit breaker policies
public HttpResponseMessage ExecuteWithRetryandCircuitBreaker(string uri,
Func<HttpResponseMessage> func)
{

    var res = _retryPolicy.Wrap(_circuitBreakerPolicy).Execute(() => func());
    return res;
}
```

We will call this method from our GET, POST, PUT, and DELETE implementation and
define the code that will be executed within the retry and circuit breaker policies.

Here is the implementation for the GET, POST, PUT, and DELETE methods, respectively:

```
public HttpResponseMessage Get(string uri)
{
    //Invoke ExecuteWithRetryandCircuitBreaker method that wraps the code
    //with retry and circuit breaker policies
    return ExecuteWithRetryandCircuitBreaker(uri, () =>
```

```
    {
      try
      {
        var requestMessage = new HttpRequestMessage(HttpMethod.Get, uri);
        var response = _client.SendAsync(requestMessage).Result;
        return response;
      }
      catch(Exception ex)
      {
        //Handle exception and return InternalServerError as response code
        HttpResponseMessage res = new HttpResponseMessage();
        res.StatusCode = HttpStatusCode.InternalServerError;
        return res;
      }
    });
  }

  //To do HTTP POST request
  public HttpResponseMessage Post<T>(string uri, T item)
  {
    //Invoke ExecuteWithRetryandCircuitBreaker method that wraps the code
    //with retry and circuit breaker policies
    return ExecuteWithRetryandCircuitBreaker(uri, () =>
    {
      try
      {
        var requestMessage = new HttpRequestMessage(HttpMethod.Post, uri);

        requestMessage.Content = new
StringContent(JsonConvert.SerializeObject(item),
        System.Text.Encoding.UTF8, "application/json");

        var response = _client.SendAsync(requestMessage).Result;

        return response;
      }catch (Exception ex)
      {
        //Handle exception and return InternalServerError as response code
        HttpResponseMessage res = new HttpResponseMessage();
        res.StatusCode = HttpStatusCode.InternalServerError;
        return res;
      }
    });
  }

  //To do HTTP PUT request
  public HttpResponseMessage Put<T>(string uri, T item)
  {
```

```
    //Invoke ExecuteWithRetryandCircuitBreaker method that wraps
    //the code with retry and circuit breaker policies
    return ExecuteWithRetryandCircuitBreaker(uri, () =>
    {
      try
      {
        var requestMessage = new HttpRequestMessage(HttpMethod.Put, uri);

        requestMessage.Content = new
StringContent(JsonConvert.SerializeObject(item),
        System.Text.Encoding.UTF8, "application/json");

        var response = _client.SendAsync(requestMessage).Result;

        return response;
      }
      catch (Exception ex)
      {
      //Handle exception and return InternalServerError as response code
      HttpResponseMessage res = new HttpResponseMessage();
      res.StatusCode = HttpStatusCode.InternalServerError;
      return res;
      }

    });
}

//To do HTTP DELETE request
public HttpResponseMessage Delete(string uri)
{
  //Invoke ExecuteWithRetryandCircuitBreaker method that wraps the code
  //with retry and circuit breaker policies
  return ExecuteWithRetryandCircuitBreaker(uri, () =>
  {
    try
    {
      var requestMessage = new HttpRequestMessage(HttpMethod.Delete, uri);

      var response = _client.SendAsync(requestMessage).Result;

      return response;

    }
    catch (Exception ex)
    {
      //Handle exception and return InternalServerError as response code
      HttpResponseMessage res = new HttpResponseMessage();
      res.StatusCode = HttpStatusCode.InternalServerError;
```

```
        return res;
    }
  });

}
```

Finally, in our startup class, we will add the dependencies as follows:

```
public void ConfigureServices(IServiceCollection services)
{

  var circuitBreakerPolicy = Policy.HandleResult<HttpResponseMessage>(x=> {
    var result = !x.IsSuccessStatusCode;
    return result;
  })
  .CircuitBreaker(3, TimeSpan.FromSeconds(60), OnBreak, OnReset,
OnHalfOpen);

    services.AddSingleton<HttpClient>();
  services.AddSingleton<CircuitBreakerPolicy<HttpResponseMessage>>(circuitBre
akerPolicy);
    services.AddSingleton<IResilientHttpClient, ResilientHttpClient>();
    services.AddMvc();
    services.AddSwaggerGen(c =>
    {
      c.SwaggerDoc("v1", new Info { Title = "User Service", Version = "v1"
});
    });
  }
```

In our `UserController` class, we can inject our custom `ResilientHttpClient` object through DI and modify the POST method, which is shown as follows:

```
[Route("api/[controller]")]
public class UserController : Controller
{

  IResilientHttpClient _resilientClient;

  HttpClient _client;
  CircuitBreakerPolicy<HttpResponseMessage> _circuitBreakerPolicy;
  public UserController(HttpClient client, IResilientHttpClient
resilientClient)
  {
    _client = client;
    _resilientClient = resilientClient;

  }
```

```
// POST api/values
[HttpPost]
public async Task<IActionResult> Post([FromBody]User user)
{

  //Email service URL
  string emailService = "http://localhost:80/api/Email";

  var response = _resilientClient.Post(emailService, user);
  if (response.IsSuccessStatusCode)
  {
    var result = response.Content.ReadAsStringAsync();
    return Ok(result);
  }

  return StatusCode((int)response.StatusCode,
response.Content.ReadAsStringAsync());
  }
}
```

With this implementation, the circuit will be initially closed when the application starts. When the request is made to the EmailService, if the service does not respond, it will try to call the service three times, waiting for three seconds on each request. If the service doesn't respond, the circuit will become open and for all subsequent requests, will stop calling the email service and will return the exception to the user for 60 seconds, as specified in the circuit breaker policy. After 60 seconds, the next request will be made to the EmailService and the circuit breaker state will be changed to Half-open. If it responds, the circuit state becomes closed again; otherwise, it remains in an open state for the next 60 seconds.

Fallback policy with circuit breaker and retry

Polly also provides a fallback policy that returns some default responses if the service is failing. It can be used in conjunction with both the retry and circuit breaker policies. The basic idea behind fallback is to send a default response to the consumer rather than returning the actual error in the response. The response should give some meaningful information to the user that is specific to the application's nature. This is very beneficial when your services are used by external consumers of applications.

We can modify the preceding example and add fallback policies for both the retry and circuit breaker exceptions. In the `ResilientHttpClient` class, we will add these two variables:

```
static FallbackPolicy<HttpResponseMessage> _fallbackPolicy;
static FallbackPolicy<HttpResponseMessage> _fallbackCircuitBreakerPolicy;
```

Next, we add the circuit breaker policy to handle the circuit breaker exception and return the `HttpResponseMessage` with our custom content message. Add the following code in the parameterized constructor of the `ResilientHttpClient` class:

```
_fallbackCircuitBreakerPolicy = Policy<HttpResponseMessage>
.Handle<BrokenCircuitException>()
.Fallback(new HttpResponseMessage(HttpStatusCode.OK)
   {
     Content = new StringContent("Please try again later[Circuit breaker is
Open]")
   }
);
```

Then, we will add another fallback policy, which will wrap the circuit breaker to handle any other exceptions that are not circuit breaker exceptions:

```
_fallbackPolicy = Policy.HandleResult<HttpResponseMessage>(r =>
r.StatusCode == HttpStatusCode.InternalServerError)
.Fallback(new HttpResponseMessage(HttpStatusCode.OK) {
  Content = new StringContent("Some error occured")
});
```

Finally, we will modify the `ExecuteWithRetryandCircuitBreaker` method and wrap both the retry and circuit breaker policy inside the fallback policies, which returns the general message with the 200 status code to the user:

```
public HttpResponseMessage ExecuteWithRetryandCircuitBreaker(string uri,
Func<HttpResponseMessage> func)
{

  PolicyWrap<HttpResponseMessage> resiliencePolicyWrap =
  Policy.Wrap(_retryPolicy, _circuitBreakerPolicy);

  PolicyWrap<HttpResponseMessage> fallbackPolicyWrap =
  _fallbackPolicy.Wrap(_fallbackCircuitBreakerPolicy.Wrap(resiliencePolicyWra
p));

  var res = fallbackPolicyWrap.Execute(() => func());
  return res;
}
```

With this implementation, the user will not get any errors in response. The content contains the actual error, which is shown in the following snapshot, taken from Fiddler:

```
☐ JSON
        asyncState=(null)
        creationOptions=0
        exception=(null)
        id=96
        isCanceled=False
        isCompleted=True
        isCompletedSuccessfully=True
        isFaulted=False
        result=Please try again later[Circuit breaker is Open]
        status=5
```

Proactive policies

According to the proactive policy, we should proactively respond to a request if it is leading towards a failure. We can use techniques such as timeout, caching, and health checks to proactively monitor application performance, and use them to proactively respond in the event of failure.

- **Timeout**: If a request takes more than the usual time, it ends the request
- **Caching**: Caches previous responses and uses them for future requests
- **Health checks**: Monitor the application's performance and invokes alerts in the event of failure

Implementing timeout

Timeout is a proactive policy, which is applicable in scenarios where the target service takes a long time to respond, and rather than letting the client wait for a response, we return a general message or response. We can use the same Polly framework to define the timeout policy, and it can also be used with the combination of retry and circuit breaker patterns we learned earlier:

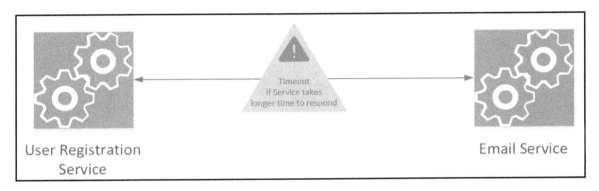

In the preceding diagram, the user registration service is calling the email service to send emails. Now, if the email service does not respond in a particular amount of time, as specified in the timeout policy, the timeout exception will be raised.

To add a timeout policy, declare a _timeoutPolicy variable in the ResilientHttpClient class:

```
static TimeoutPolicy<HttpResponseMessage> _timeoutPolicy;
```

Then, add the following code to initialize the timeout policy:

```
_timeoutPolicy = Policy.Timeout<HttpResponseMessage>(1);
```

Finally, we will wrap the timeout policy and add it in resiliencyPolicyWrap. Here is the modified code of the ExecuteWithRetryandCircuitBreaker method:

```
public HttpResponseMessage ExecuteWithRetryandCircuitBreaker(string uri,
Func<HttpResponseMessage> func)
{

  PolicyWrap<HttpResponseMessage> resiliencePolicyWrap =
  Policy.Wrap(_timeoutPolicy, _retryPolicy, _circuitBreakerPolicy);

  PolicyWrap<HttpResponseMessage> fallbackPolicyWrap =
  _fallbackPolicy.Wrap(_fallbackCircuitBreakerPolicy.Wrap(resiliencePolicyWra
```

```
  p));

    var res = fallbackPolicyWrap.Execute(() => func());
    return res;
}
```

Implementing caching

When making a web request or calling a remote service, Polly can be used to cache the response from the remote service and improve the performance of the application's response time. The Polly cache is classified into two caches, known as the in-memory cache and the distributed cache. We will configure the in-memory cache in this section.

First, we need to add another `Polly.Caching.MemoryCache` package from NuGet. Once this is added, we will modify our `Startup` class and add the `IPolicyRegistry` as a member variable:

```
private IPolicyRegistry<string> _registry;
```

In the `ConfigurationServices` method, we will initialize the registry and add it as a singleton object through DI:

```
_registry = new PolicyRegistry();
services.AddSingleton(_registry);
```

In the configure method, we will define the cache policy that takes the cache provider and the time to cache the responses. Since we are using in-memory cache, we will initialize the memory cache provider and specify it in the policy as follows:

```
Polly.Caching.MemoryCache.MemoryCacheProvider memoryCacheProvider = new
MemoryCacheProvider(memoryCache);

CachePolicy<HttpResponseMessage> cachePolicy =
Policy.Cache<HttpResponseMessage>(memoryCacheProvider,
TimeSpan.FromMinutes(10));
```

Finally, we will add the `cachepolicy` to our registry, which is initialized in the `ConfigurationServices` method. We named our registry `cache`:

```
_registry.Add("cache", cachePolicy);
```

Modify our `UserController` class and declare the generic `CachePolicy` as follows:

```
CachePolicy<HttpResponseMessage> _cachePolicy;
```

We will now modify our `UserController` constructor and add the registry, which will be injected through the DI. This registry object is used to get the cache defined in the `Configure` method.

Here is the modified constructor of the `UserController` class:

```
public UserController(HttpClient client, IResilientHttpClient
resilientClient, IPolicyRegistry<string> registry)
{
  _client = client;
  // _circuitBreakerPolicy = circuitBreakerPolicy;
  _resilientClient = resilientClient;

  _cachePolicy = registry.Get<CachePolicy<HttpResponseMessage>>("cache");
}
```

Finally, we will define a GET method that calls another service to get the list of users and cache it in the memory. To cache the responses, we will wrap our custom resilient client GET method with the `Execute` method of the cache policy as follows:

```
[HttpGet]
public async Task<IActionResult> Get()
{
  //Specify the name of the Response. If the method is taking
  //parameter, we can append the actual parameter to cache unique
  //responses separately
  Context policyExecutionContext = new Context($"GetUsers");

  var response = _cachePolicy.Execute(()=>
  _resilientClient.Get("http://localhost:7637/api/users"),
policyExecutionContext);
  if (response.IsSuccessStatusCode)
  {
    var result = response.Content.ReadAsStringAsync();
    return Ok(result);
  }

  return StatusCode((int)response.StatusCode,
response.Content.ReadAsStringAsync());
}
```

When the request is returned, it will check whether the cache context is empty or expired, and the request will be cached for 10 minutes. All subsequent requests during that time will read the response from the in-memory cache store. Once the cache has expired, based on the set time limit, it will invoke the remote service again and cache the response.

Implementing health checks

Health checks are part of the proactive strategy, where the services' health can be monitored in a timely fashion. They also allow you to take actions proactively if any service is not responding or is in a failure state.

In ASP.NET Core, we can easily implement health checks by using the `HealthChecks` library, which is available as a NuGet package. To use `HealthChecks`, we can just simply add the following NuGet package to our ASP.NET Core MVC or Web API project:

`Microsoft.AspNetCore.HealthChecks`

We have to add this package to the application that monitors the services and the services whose health needs to be monitored.

Add the following code in the `ConfigureServices` method of the `Startup` class of the application that is used to check the health of services:

```
services.AddHealthChecks(checks =>
{
  checks.AddUrlCheck(Configuration["UserServiceURL"]);
  checks.AddUrlCheck(Configuration["EmailServiceURL"]);
});
```

In the preceding code, we have added two service endpoints to check the health status. These endpoints are defined in the `appsettings.json` file.

The health check library checks the health of the services specified using the `AddUrlCheck` method. However, the services whose health needs to be monitored by external applications or services need some modification in the `Startup` class. We have to add the following code snippet to all of the services to return their health status:

```
services.AddHealthChecks(checks =>
{
  checks.AddValueTaskCheck("HTTP Endpoint", () => new
  ValueTask<IHealthCheckResult>(HealthCheckResult.Healthy("Ok")));
});
```

If their health is good and the service is responding, it will return Ok.

Finally, we can add the URI in the monitoring application, which will trigger the health check middleware to check the services' health and display the health status. We have to add UseHealthChecks and specify the endpoint used to trigger the services' health status:

```
public static IWebHost BuildWebHost(string[] args) =>
WebHost.CreateDefaultBuilder(args)
.UseHealthChecks("/hc")
.UseStartup<Startup>()
.Build();
```

When we run our monitoring application and access the URI, for example, http://{base_address}/hc to get the health status, if all the services are in working order, we should see the following response:

Storing sensitive information using Application Secrets

Every application has some configuration holding sensitive information, such as database connection strings, the secret keys of some third providers, and other sensitive information usually stored in the configuration files or the database. It is always a better option to secure all sensitive information to protect these resources from intruders. Web applications are usually hosted on servers, and this information can be read by just navigating to the server's path and accessing files, even though servers always have protected access and only authorized users are eligible to access the data. However, keeping information in plain text is not a good practice.

In .NET Core, we can use the Secret Manager tool to protect the sensitive information of an application. The Secret Manager tool allows you to store information in a secrets.json file, which is not stored within the application folder itself. Instead, that file is saved at the following path for different platforms:

```
Windows: %APPDATA%microsoftUserSecrets{userSecretsId}secrets.json
Linux: ~/.microsoft/usersecrets/{userSecretsId}/secrets.json
Mac: ~/.microsoft/usersecrets/{userSecretsId}/secrets.json
```

{userSecretId} is the unique ID (GUID) associated with your application. Since this is saved in the separate path, each developer has to define or create this file in their own directory under the UserSecrets directory. This restricts the developer from checking in the same file for the source control and keeps the information separate to each user. There are scenarios where a developer uses their own account credentials for database authentication and so this facilitates in keeping certain information isolated from other information.

From Visual Studio, we can simply add the secrets.json file by right-clicking on the project and selecting the **Manage User Secrets** option, which is shown as follows:

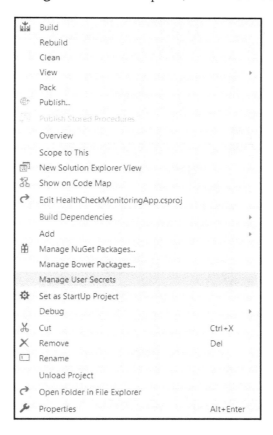

When you select **Manage User Secrets**, Visual Studio creates a `secrets.json` file and opens it in Visual Studio to add configuration settings in JSON format. If you open the project file, you see the entry of the `UserSecretsId` stored in your project file:

```xml
<Project Sdk="Microsoft.NET.Sdk.Web">

  <PropertyGroup>
    <TargetFramework>netcoreapp2.0</TargetFramework>
    <UserSecretsId>de247bd5-6f82-45ac-b8d4-645428545fff</UserSecretsId>
  </PropertyGroup>
```

So, if you accidently close the `secrets.json` file, you can open it from the path where `UserSecretsId` is the subfolder inside the user secrets path, which is shown in the preceding screenshot.

Here is the sample content of the `secrets.json` file that contains the logging information, remote services URL, and the connection string:

```json
{
  "Logging": {
    "IncludeScopes": false,
    "Debug": {
      "LogLevel": {
        "Default": "Warning"
      }
    },
    "Console": {
      "LogLevel": {
        "Default": "Warning"
      }
    }
  },
  "EmailServiceURL": "http://localhost:6670/api/values",
  "UserServiceURL": "http://localhost:6546/api/user",
  "ConnectionString": "Server=OVAISPC\sqlexpress;Database=FraymsVendorDB;
  User Id=sa;Password=P@ssw0rd;"
}
```

To access this in the ASP.NET Core application, we can add the following namespace in our `Startup` class:

```
using Microsoft.Extensions.Configuration;
```

Then, inject the `IConfiguration` object and assign it to the `Configuration` property:

```
public Startup(IConfiguration configuration)
{
  Configuration = configuration;
}
public IConfiguration Configuration { get; }
```

Finally, we can access the variables using the `Configuration` object as follows:

```
var UserServicesURL = Configuration["UserServiceURL"]
services.AddEntityFrameworkSqlServer()
.AddDbContext<VendorDBContext>(options =>
{
  options.UseSqlServer(Configuration["ConnectionString"],
  sqlServerOptionsAction: sqlOptions =>
  {
    sqlOptions.MigrationsAssembly(typeof(Startup)
    .GetTypeInfo().Assembly.GetName().Name);
    sqlOptions.EnableRetryOnFailure(maxRetryCount: 10,
    maxRetryDelay: TimeSpan.FromSeconds(30), errorNumbersToAdd: null);
  });
}, ServiceLifetime.Scoped
);
}
```

Protecting ASP.NET Core APIs

Securing web applications is an important milestone for any enterprise-grade application to protect not only the data, but also to protect it from different attacks from malicious sites.

There are various scenarios where security is an important factor for any web application:

- The information sent over the wire contains sensitive information.
- APIs are exposed publicly and are used by users to perform bulk operations.
- APIs are hosted on a server where the user can use some tools to do packet sniffing and read sensitive data.

To address the preceding challenges and to secure our application, we should consider the following options:

SSL (Secure Socket Layer)

Add security at the transport or network level, where when, the data is sent from the client to the server, it should be encrypted. The **SSL** (**Secure Socket Layer**) is the recommended way of securing information sent over the wire. Use SSL in a web application to encrypt all of the data that is sent from the client's browser to the server over the wire where it is decrypted at the server level. Apparently, it seems like a performance overhead, but due to the specifications of the server resources we have in today's world, it seems quite negligible.

Enabling SSL in an ASP.NET Core application

To enable SSL in our ASP.NET Core project, we can add filters in the AddMvc method defined in the ConfigureServices method of our Startup class. Filters are used to filter the HTTP calls and take certain actions:

```
services.AddMvc(options =>
{
  options.Filters.Add(new RequireHttpsAttribute())
});
```

Filters added in the AddMvc method are global filters and interrupt all HTTP requests, irrespective of a specific controller or action. We added the RequireHttpsAttribute filter, which validates the incoming request and checks whether the request is on HTTP or HTTPS. If the request is on HTTP, it will auto redirect the request to HTTPS and use the default port, which is 443 in the case of HTTPS. Adding the preceding code snippet is not enough to run our application on SSL. We also need to tell the launchSettings.json file to use the HTTPS port and enable SSL for our project. One way to do this is to enable SSL from the **Debug** tab in the Visual Studio project properties window, which is shown as follows:

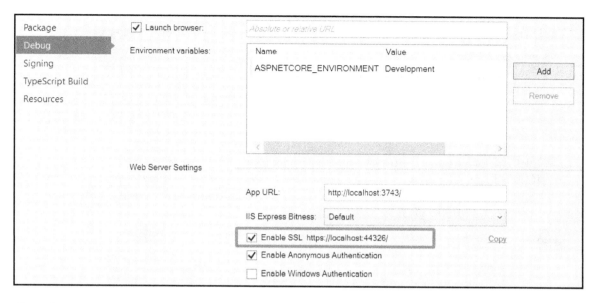

This also modifies the launchSettings.json file and adds the SSL. Another way is to directly modify the port number from the launchSetttings.json file itself. Here is the launchsettings.json file that uses port 44326 for SSL, which has been added under iisSettings:

```
{
  "iisSettings": {
    "windowsAuthentication": false,
    "anonymousAuthentication": true,
    "iisExpress": {
      "applicationUrl": "http://localhost:3743/",
      "sslPort": 44326
    }
  },
```

The default HTTP port, which is shown in the preceding code, is set to *3743*. As in the AddMvc middleware, we have specified a filter to use SSL for all incoming requests. It will automatically redirect to the HTTPS and use port 44326.

To host ASP.NET Core on IIS, please refer to the following link. Once the website is up and running, the HTTPS binding can be added through the Site bindings options in IIS: https://docs.microsoft.com/en-us/aspnet/core/host-and-deploy/iis/index?tabs=aspnetcore2x

Preventing CSRF (Cross-Site Request Forgery) attacks

CSRF is an attack that executes unsolicited operations on a web application on behalf of the authenticated user. Since the attacker is unable to forge the response of the request, it is implicated mostly on HTTP POST, PUT, and DELETE methods, which are used to modify the insert, update, or delete data on the server.

ASP.NET Core provides a built-in token to prevent CSRF attacks, and you can do this yourself by adding the ValidateAntiForgeryTokenAttribute filter while adding MVC in the ConfigureServices method of the Startup class. Here is the code to add an anti-forgery token globally to your ASP.NET Core application:

```
public void ConfigureServices(IServiceCollection services)
{
services.AddMvc(options => { options.Filters.Add(new
ValidateAntiForgeryTokenAttribute()); });
  }
```

Alternatively, we can also add ValidateAntyForgeryToken on specific controller action methods. In that case, we don't have to add the ValidateAntiForgeryTokenAttribute filter in the ConfigureServices method of the Startup class. Here is the code to protect the HTTP POST action method from CSRF attacks:

```
[HttpPost]

[ValidateAntiForgeryToken]
public async Task<IActionResult> Submit()
{
   return View();
}
CORS (Cross Origin Security)
```

The second option is to enable CORS (Cross-Origin Security) for authenticated origins, headers, and methods. Setting CORS allows your APIs to be only accessible from configured origins. In ASP.NET Core, CORS can be easily set by adding middleware and defining its policy.

The ValidateAntiForgery attribute tells ASP.NET Core to put the token in the form, and when it's submitted, it validates and ensures that the token is valid. This prevents your application from CSRF attacks by validating the token for every HTTP POST, PUT, and other HTTP requests, and protects the forms from being posted maliciously.

Reinforcing security headers

Many modern browsers provide additional security features. These security features are automatically enabled by the browser running your site if the response contains those headers. In this section, we will discuss how we can add those headers in our ASP.NET Core application and enable additional security in the browser.

To investigate which headers are missing in our application, we can use the `www.SecurityHeaders.io` site. However, to use this, we need our site to be publicly accessible on the internet.

Alternatively, we can use `ngrok` to make a HTTP tunnel to our local application, which makes our site accessible from the internet. The `ngrok` tool can be downloaded from the following link: `https://ngrok.com/download`.

You can select the version of OS you have and download a particular installer accordingly.

Once `ngrok` is installed, you can open it and the run following command. Please note that your site should be running locally before executing the following command:

```
ngrok http -host-header localhost 7204
```

You can replace `localhost` with your server IP and `7204` to the port your application is listening on.

Running the preceding command will generate the public URL, as specified in the `Forwarding` property, as follows:

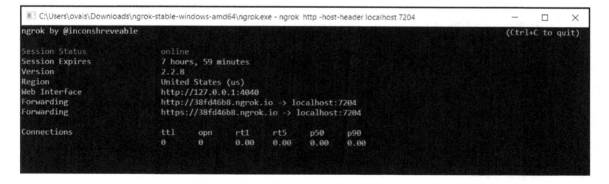

We can now use this public URL in `www.securityheaders.io`, which scans our site and gives us the result. It categorizes the site and provides an alphabet starting from A to F, where A is an excellent score that means the site contains all security headers, and F means that the site is not secure and does not contain security headers. Scanning the default ASP.NET Core site generated from the default template scored F, which is shown as follows. It also shows the missing headers, which are boxed in red:

First of all, we should enable HTTPS on our site. To enable HTTPS, please refer to the section related to SSL. Next, we will add the `NWebsec.AspNetCore.Middleware` package from NuGet as follows:

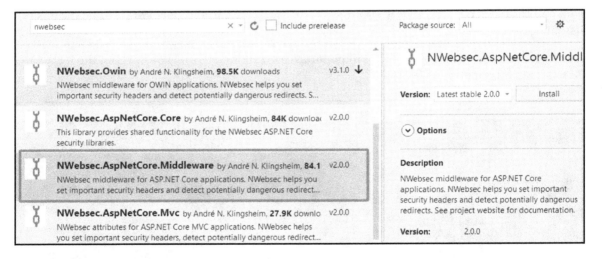

NWebsec comes with various **middleware** that can be added to our application from the `Configure` method of the `Startup` class.

Adding the HTTP strict transport security header

The strict transport security header is an excellent feature that strengthens the implementation of **TLS (Transport Level Security)** by getting the **User Agent** and forcing it to use HTTPS. We can add the strict transport security header by adding the following middleware to our `Configure` method of the `Startup` class:

```
app.UseHsts(options => options.MaxAge(days:365).IncludeSubdomains());
```

This middleware enforces your site so that it can only be accessed over HTTPS for a year. This applies to subdomains as well.

Adding the X-Content-Type-Options header

This header stops a browser from trying to `MIME-sniff` the content type and forces it to stick with the declared content-type. We can add this middleware as follows, in the `Configure` method of the `Startup` class:

```
app.UseXContentTypeOptions();
```

Adding the X-Frame-Options header

This header allows the browser to protect your site from being rendered inside a frame. By using the following middleware, we can prevent our site from framing so that we can defend it against different attacks, where the most famous one is clickjacking:

```
app.UseXfo(options => options.SameOrigin());
```

Adding the X-Xss-Protection header

This header allows the browser to stop pages from loading when they detect Cross Site scripting attacks. We can add this middleware in the `Configure` method of the `Startup` class, as follows:

```
app.UseXXssProtection(options => options.EnabledWithBlockMode());
```

Adding the Content-Security-Policy header

The *Content-Security-Policy* header protects your application by whitelisting the sources of approved content and preventing the browser from loading malicious resources. This can be added by adding the `NWebsec.Owin` package from NuGet and defining it in the `Configure` method of the `Startup` class as follows:

```
app.UseCsp(options => options
.DefaultSources(s => s.Self())
.ScriptSources(s => s.Self()));
```

In the preceding code, we have mentioned the `DefaultSources` and `ScriptSources` to load all the resources from the same origin. If there are any scripts or images that need to be loaded from external sources, we can define the custom sources as follows:

```
app.UseCsp(options => options
    .DefaultSources(s => s.Self()).ScriptSources(s =>
s.Self().CustomSources("https://ajax.googleapis.com")));
```

For the complete documentation on this topic, please refer to the following URL: `https://docs.nwebsec.com/en/4.1/nwebsec/Configuring-csp.html`.

Adding the referrer-policy header

When a user navigates the site and click links to other sites, the destination site usually receives information about the origin site the user came from. The referrer header lets you control what information should be present in the header, which can be read by the destination site. We can add the referrer policy middleware in the `Configure` method of the `Startup` class as follows:

```
app.UseReferrerPolicy(opts => opts.NoReferrer());
```

The `NoReferrer` option means that no referrer information will be sent to the target site.

After enabling all of the preceding middleware in our ASP.NET Core application, when we scan through the `securityheaders.io` site, we will see that we have a security report summary with an **A+**, which means that the site is completely secured:

Enabling CORS in the ASP.NET Core application

CORS stands for Cross-Origin Resource Sharing, and it is restricted by browsers to prevent API requests across domains. For example, we have an SPA (Single-Page Application) running on a browser using a client-side framework like Angular or React to make calls to the Web APIs hosted on another domain, like my SPA site having a domain (*mychapter8webapp.com*) and accessing the APIs of another domain (`appservices.com`), which is restricted. Making calls to the services hosted on some other server and domain is restricted by browsers, and users will not be able to call those APIs. Enabling CORS on the server-side level addresses this problem.

To enable CORS in our ASP.NET Core project, we can add CORS support in the `ConfigureServices` method:

```
services.AddCors();
```

In the `Configure` method, we can use CORS by calling the `UseCors` method and defining the policies to allow cross-domain requests. The following code allows requests to be made from any header, origin, or method, and also allows us to pass credentials in the request header:

```
app.UseCors(config => {
  config.AllowAnyHeader();
  config.AllowAnyMethod();
  config.AllowAnyOrigin();
  config.AllowCredentials();
});
```

The preceding code will allow CORS globally in the application. Alternatively, we can also define CORS policies and enable them on specific controllers depending on different scenarios.

The following table defines the basic terminology used in defining CORS:

Terminology	Description	Sample
Header	Request header allowed to be passed within the request	Content-Type, Accept, and so on
Method	HTTP verb of the request	GET, POST, DELETE, PUT, and so on
Origin	Domain or request URL	http://techframeworx.com

To define the policies, we can add a policy when adding CORS support in the `ConfigureServices` method. The following code shows two policies that have been defined while adding CORS support:

```
services.AddCors(config =>
{
  //Allow only HTTP GET Requests
  config.AddPolicy("AllowOnlyGet", builder =>
  {
    builder.AllowAnyHeader();
    builder.WithMethods("GET");
    builder.AllowAnyOrigin();
  });

  //Allow only those requests coming from techframeworx.com
  config.AddPolicy("Techframeworx", builder => {
    builder.AllowAnyHeader();
    builder.AllowAnyMethod();
    builder.WithOrigins("http://techframeworx.com");
  });
});
```

The `AllowOnlyGet` policy will only allow requests that are making a GET request; the `Techframeworx` policy will only allow requests that are being made from techframeworx.com.

We can use these policies on Controllers and Actions by using the `EnableCors` attribute and specifying the name of the attribute:

```
[EnableCors("AllowOnlyGet")]
public class SampleController : Controller
{
```

```
}
```

Authentication and authorization

Secure APIs only allow access to authenticated users. In ASP.NET Core, we can use the ASP.NET Core Identity framework to authenticate users and provide authorized access to protected resources.

Using ASP.NET Core Identity for authentication and authorization

Security, in general, is divided into two mechanisms, which are as follows:

- Authentication
- Authorization

Authentication

Authentication is the process of authenticating the user's access by getting their username, password, or authentication token and then validating it from the backend database or service. Once the user is authenticated, certain actions are done, which involves setting up a cookie in the browser or returning a token to the user so that it can be passed in the request message to access protected resources.

Authorization

Authorization is the process that is done after user authentication. Authorization is used to learn the permissions of the user accessing the resource. Even though the user is authenticated, it does not mean that all the protected or secured resources are accessible. This is where authorization comes into play and only allows the user to access resources that they are permitted to access.

Implementing authentication and authorization using the ASP.NET Core Identity framework

ASP.NET Core Identity is the security framework developed by Microsoft and is now contributed to by the open source community. This allows a developer to enable user authentication and authorization in an ASP.NET Core application. It provides the complete system of storing user identities, roles, and claims in a database. It contains certain classes for user identity, roles, and so on, which can be extended further to support more properties, depending on the requirements. It uses Entity Framework Core code for the first model to create the backend database and can be easily integrated with existing data models or the application's specific tables.

In this section, we will create a simple application to add ASP.NET Core Identity from scratch and modify the `IdentityUser` class to define additional properties and use cookie-based authentication to validate requests and secure ASP.NET MVC controllers.

When creating an ASP.NET Core project, we can change the authentication option to **Individual User Account** authentication, which scaffolds all the security-specific classes and configures security in your application:

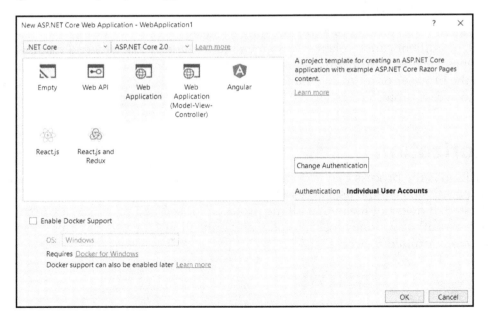

This creates an `AccountController` and `PageModels` to register, login, forgot password, and other user management-related pages.

The `Startup` class also contains some entries related to security. Here is the `ConfigureServices` method, which adds some code that is specific to security:

```
public void ConfigureServices(IServiceCollection services)
{
    services.AddDbContext<ApplicationDbContext>(options =>
    options.UseSqlServer(Configuration.GetConnectionString("DefaultConnection")
    ));

    services.AddIdentity<ApplicationUser, IdentityRole>()
    .AddEntityFrameworkStores<ApplicationDbContext>()
    .AddDefaultTokenProviders();

    services.AddMvc()
    .AddRazorPagesOptions(options =>
    {
        options.Conventions.AuthorizeFolder("/Account/Manage");
        options.Conventions.AuthorizePage("/Account/Logout");
    });

    services.AddSingleton<IEmailSender, EmailSender>();
}
```

`AddDbContext` uses the SQL server to create Identity tables in the database, as specified in the `DefaultConnection` key as follows:

- `services.AddIdentity` is used to enable Identity in our application. It takes `ApplicationUser` and `IdentityRole` and defines `ApplicationDbContext` to use as the Entity framework, which is used to store the created entities.
- `AddDefaultTokenProviders` is defined to generate tokens for reset passwords, changing email, changing telephone number, and two-factor authentication.

In the `Configure` method, it adds the `UseAuthentication` middleware, which enables the authentication and protects the pages or controllers that are configured to authorize requests. Here is the `Configure` method that enables authentication in the pipeline. The middleware which is defined is executed in a sequence. Therefore, the `UseAuthentication` middleware is defined before the `UseMvc` middleware so that all of the requests that will be invoking the controllers will be authenticated first:

```
public void Configure(IApplicationBuilder app, IHostingEnvironment env)
{
    if (env.IsDevelopment())
```

```
    {
      app.UseBrowserLink();
      app.UseDeveloperExceptionPage();
      app.UseDatabaseErrorPage();
    }
    else
    {
      app.UseExceptionHandler("/Error");
    }

    app.UseStaticFiles();

    app.UseAuthentication();

    app.UseMvc();
}
```

Adding more properties in the user table

`IdentityUser` is the base class, which contains properties such as email, password, and phone number, which are related to the user. When we create the ASP.NET Core application, it creates an empty `ApplicationUser` class that inherits from the `IdentityUser` class. In the `ApplicationUser` class, we can add more properties that will be created once the entity framework migration is run. We will add `FirstName`, `LastName`, and `MobileNumber` properties in our `ApplicationUser` class, which will be considered when the table is created:

```
public class ApplicationUser : IdentityUser
{
  public string FirstName { get; set; }
  public string LastName { get; set; }
  public string MobileNumber { get; set; }
}
```

Before running the migration, make sure that the `DefaultConnection` string specified in the `ConfigureServices` method of the `Startup` class is valid.

We can run the migration from the **Package Manager Console** in Visual Studio or through the *dotnet CLI* toolset. From Visual Studio, select the specific project and run the `Add-Migration` command, specifying the migration name, which is Initial in our case:

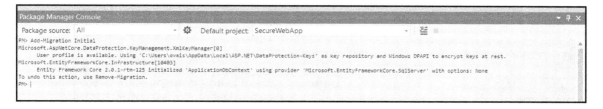

The preceding command creates the `{timestamp}_Initial` class file containing the `Up` and `Down` methods. The `Up` method is used to publish the changes in the backend database, whereas the `Down` method is used to revert the changes done in the database. To apply the changes to the backend database, we will run the `Update-Database` command, which creates a database that contains `AspNet`-related tables, which are part of the Identity framework. If you open the `AspNetUsers` table in design mode, you will see that the custom columns `FirstName`, `LastName`, and `MobileNumber` are there:

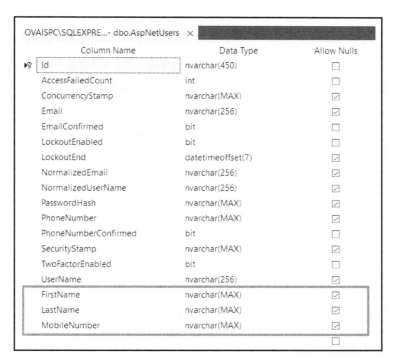

We can run the application and create users using the **Register** option. To protect our APIs, we have to add the `Authorize` attribute to the `Controller` or `Action` level. When the request comes and the user is authenticated, the method will be executed; otherwise, it redirects the request to the **Login** page.

Summary

In this chapter, we have learned about resiliency, which is a very important factor when developing highly performant applications in .NET Core. We learned about different policies and used the Polly framework to use those policies in .NET Core. We also learned about safe storage mechanisms and how to use them in a development environment in order to keep sensitive information separate from the project repository. At the end of this chapter, we learned about some core fundamentals, which included SSL, CSRF, CORS, enabling security headers, and the ASP.NET Core Identity framework to protect ASP.NET Core applications.

In the next chapter, we will learn about some key metrics and necessary tools to monitor the performance of .NET Core applications.

Microservices Architecture

8

Microservices application development is growing at a rapid pace in the software industry. It is widely used for developing performant applications that are resilient, scalable, distributed, and cloud-ready. Many organizations and software companies are transforming their applications into the microservices architecture style. Amazon, eBay, and Uber are good examples of companies that have transformed their applications into microservices.

Microservices split the application horizontally and vertically into smaller components, where the components are independent of one another and communicate through an endpoint. With the recent development in the industry of containers, we can use containers to deploy/run microservices that can scale up or scale out independently without any dependency on other components of the application and are leveraged with the pay-as-you-go model.

Today, we can use **Azure Container Service (ACS)** or Service Fabric to deploy .NET Core applications in the cloud and provide a containerization model with the consortium of Docker, Kubernetes, and other third-party components.

In this chapter, we will learn the fundamentals of microservices architecture and its challenges, and create a basic application following microservices principles and practices.

The following are the topics we will learn in this chapter:

- Microservices architecture
- Benefits and standard practices
- Stateless versus stateful microservices
- Decomposing databases and its challenges
- Developing microservices in .NET Core
- Running .NET Core microservices on Docker

Microservices architecture

Microservices architecture is an architectural style in which the application is loosely coupled; it is divided into components based on business capability or domain, and scales independently without affecting other services or components of the application. This contrasts with the monolithic architecture, where a full application is deployed on a server or a **Virtual Machine** (**VM**) and scaling out is not a cost-effective or easy solution. For each scale-out operation, a new VM instance has to be cloned and the application needs to be deployed.

The following diagram shows the architecture of a monolithic application, where most of the functionality is isolated within a single process and scaling out to multiple servers requires the full deployment of the application on the other server:

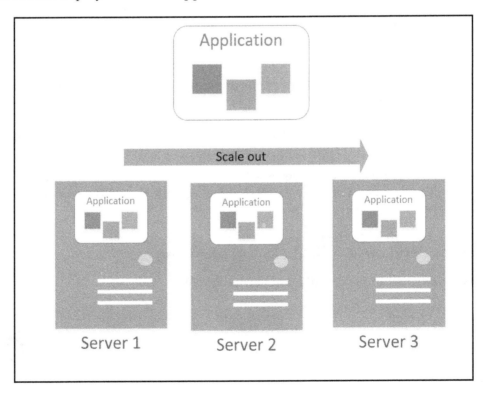

The following is a representation of microservices architecture, which separates an application into smaller services and, based on the workload, scales independently:

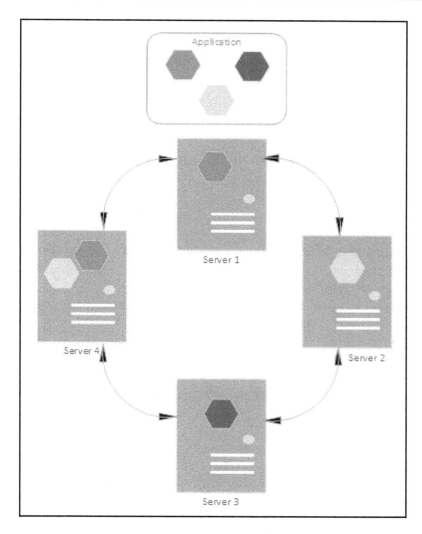

In microservices architecture, the application is divided into loosely coupled services, each of which exposes an endpoint and is deployed on a separate server or, most likely, container. Each service communicates with the other services through some endpoint.

Benefits of microservices architecture

There are various benefits of microservices architecture, which are as follows:

- Microservices are autonomous and expose a self-contained unit of functionality with loosely coupled dependencies on other services
- It exposes features to a caller via a well-defined API contract
- It degrades gracefully if any service fails
- It scales up and scales out independently
- It is best suited for containerized deployment, which is a cost-effective solution when compared to VMs
- Each component can be reused through an endpoint and modifying any service does not affect other services
- Development is faster when compared to monolithic architecture
- As each microservice provides a particular business capability, it is easily reusable and composable
- As each service is independent, using old architecture or technology is not a concern.
- It is resilient and eliminates monolith failover scenarios

Standard practice when developing microservices

As standard practice, microservices are designed and decomposed based on business capability or business domain. Business domain decomposition follows a **Domain-Driven Design** (**DDD**) pattern, where each service is developed to provide specific functionality of the business domain. This contrasts with a layered architecture approach, in which the application is divided into multiple layers, where each layer is dependent on another layer and has tight dependencies on it, and removing any layer breaks the whole application.

The following diagram illustrates the difference between layered architecture and microservices architecture:

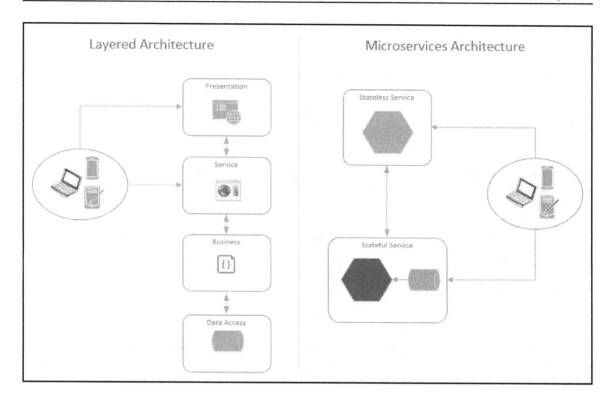

Types of microservices

Microservices are divided into two categories, which are as follows:

- Stateless microservices
- Stateful microservices

Stateless microservices

A stateless service has either no state or the state can be retrieved from an external data store. As the state is stored separately, multiple instances can run at the same time.

Stateful microservices

A stateful service maintains the state within its own context. Only a single instance is active at a time. However, the state is replicated to other inactive instances as well.

DDD

DDD is a pattern that emphasizes the business domain of the application. When building the application following a DDD pattern, we divide the application based on business domains, where each domain has one or more bounded contexts and the bounded context represents the business requirement. In technical terms, each bounded context has its own code and persistence mechanism and is independent of the others. Consider a vendor-management system where a vendor registers with the website, logs into the website, updates their profile, and attaches quotations. Each type of action will be termed the bounded context and is independent of the others. A set of vendor-operations can be termed a vendor domain.

DDD splits the requirement into domain-specific chunks known as bounded contexts, where each bounded context has its own model, logic, and data. There are chances that a single service is used by many services because of the core functionality it provides. For example, a vendor registration service uses an identity service to create a new user and the same identity service may be used by some other service to log into the system.

Data manipulation with microservices

As a general practice, each service provides specific business functionality to the user and involves **Create**, **Read**, **Update**, and **Delete** (**CRUD**) operations. In enterprise applications, we have one or more databases that have a number of tables. Following the DDD pattern, we can design each service that focuses on the specific domain. However, there are conditions where we need to extract the data from some other databases or tables that are out of scope from the service's domain. However, there are two options to address this challenge:

- Wrapping microservices behind an API gateway
- Decomposing data into a flat schema for read/query purposes

Wrapping microservices behind an API gateway

An enterprise application that is based on microservices architecture contains many services. An **Entity Resource Planning** (**ERP**) system contains many modules, such as **Human Resources** (**HR**), financial, purchase requisition, and others. Each module may have a number of services providing specific business features. For example, the HR module may contain the following three services:

- Personal record management
- Appraisal management
- Recruitment management

The personal record management service exposes certain methods to create, update, or delete an employee's basic information. The appraisal-management service exposes certain methods to create appraisal requests for an employee, and the recruitment-management service performs new hiring decisions. Suppose we need to develop a web page that contains the basic employee information and the total number of appraisals done in the last five years. In this case, we will be calling two services, namely personal-record management and appraisal management, and two separate calls will be made by the caller to these services. Alternatively, we can wrap these two calls into a single call using an API gateway. The technique to address this scenario is known as **API composition** and is discussed in the *What is API composition?* section later in the chapter.

Denormalizing data into a flat schema for read/query purposes

This is another technique where we want to consume a service to read data from heterogeneous sources. It could be from multiple tables or databases. To transform multiple service calls into a single call, we can design each service and use patterns such as publisher/subscriber or mediator that listen for any CRUD operation to be performed on any service, save the data into a flat schema, and develop a service that only reads the data from that table(s). The technique to address this scenario is known as **Command Query Responsibility Segregation** (**CQRS**) and is discussed in the CQRS section later in the chapter.

Consistency across business scenarios

As we understand that each service is designed to serve a specific business functionality, let's take an example of an order-management system where a customer comes to the website and places an order. Once the order is placed, it is reflected in the inventory. In this scenario, we can have two microservices: one that places an order and creates a database record into the order database and an inventory service that performs CRUD on the inventory-related tables:

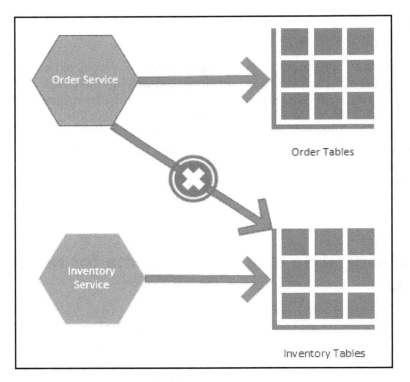

The important practice to follow when implementing an end-to-end business scenario and bringing consistency across multiple microservices is to keep the data and model specific to their domain. Considering the preceding example, the order placement service should not access or perform CRUD operations other than order tables, and if it is necessary to access any data which is out of the domain of that service, it should call that service directly.

An **Atomicity, Consistency, Integrity, and Durability (ACID)** transaction is another challenge. We may have multiple services serving one complete transaction, where each transaction is behind and operated by a separate service. To accommodate ACID transactions with the microservices architecture style, we can implement **asynchronous event-driven communication**, which is discussed later in the chapter.

Communication with microservices

In microservices architecture, each microservice is hosted at some server, most likely a container, and exposes an endpoint. These endpoints can be used to communicate to that service. There are many protocols that we can use but REST-based HTTP endpoints are most widely used due to their accessibility support on many platforms. In ASP.NET Core, we can create microservices using the ASP.NET Core MVC framework and use them through a RESTful endpoint. There are microservices that use other microservices as well to complete a particular operation and this can easily be done using the `HttpClient` class in .NET Core. However, we should design in such a way that our service offers resiliency and handles transient faults.

Database architecture in microservices

With microservices architecture, each service provides a certain functionality and has minimal dependencies on other services. However, porting the relational database into the smaller sets is a challenge, where each set represents a particular domain and contains tables related to that domain. Segregating tables based on domain and making them individual databases needs proper consideration.

Let's consider the vendor management system that provides **Business-to-Consumer (B2C)** and **Business-to-Business (B2B)** processes and involves the following operations:

- Vendor registers with the website
- Vendor adds products that can be purchased by other vendors or customers
- Vendor places orders to purchase products

To implement the preceding scenario, we can decompose the database based on the following two patterns:

- Tables per service
- Database per service

Tables per service

With this design, each service is designed to use specific tables in the database. In this scenario, the database is centralized and hosted at one place. Other microservices also connect to the same database but deal with their own domain-specific tables:

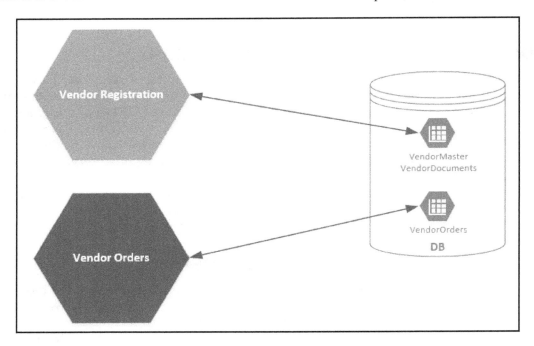

This helps us to use the central database but any modification in the schema may break or require an update for one or many microservices.

Database per service

With this design, each service has its own database and the application is loosely coupled. Modifications in the database do not harm or break any other service and offer complete isolation. This design is good for deployment scenarios, as each service contains its own database deployed in its own container:

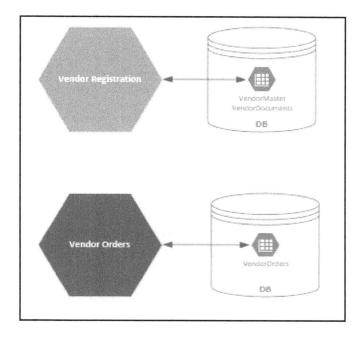

Challenges in segregating tables or databases per service

Segregating tables or databases as per business capability or business domain is recommended to limit dependencies and keep it intact with the domain model. But it also comes with some challenges. For example, we have two services: a vendor service and an order service. The vendor service is used to create a vendor record in its own vendor database, and the order service to place orders for a particular vendor. The challenge comes when we need to return the aggregated record of both the vendor and their orders to the user. To solve this problem, we can use either of the following two approaches:

- API composition
- CQRS

What is API composition?

API composition is a technique in which multiple microservices are composed to expose one endpoint to the user and provides an aggregated view. In a single database, this is easily possible by making a SQL query join and getting the data from different tables.

Let's consider the vendor management system, where we have two services. One is used to register a new vendor and has a corresponding database to persist vendor demographics, address, and other information. The other service is the order service, which is used to store the transactional data of the vendor and contains order information such as order number, quantity, and so on. Suppose we have a requirement to display the list of vendors with all the orders that are completed. With this scenario, we can provide a method in the vendor registration service that first loads the vendor details from its own data store, then loads their orders by calling the order service, and finally returns the aggregated data.

CQRS

CQRS is a principle in which application commands such as create, update, and delete are segregated by read operations. It works on the event-based model and when any create, update, or delete action is taken on the API, the event handler is invoked and stores that information into its own corresponding data store. We can implement CQRS in the previous vendor registration example, which will facilitate querying the vendor and their orders from a single service. When any command (create, update, delete) operation is performed on the vendor or order service, it will invoke the handler that invokes the query service to save the updated data into its store.

We can keep the data in a flat schema or used NoSQL database to hold all the information about the vendor and their orders and read them when required:

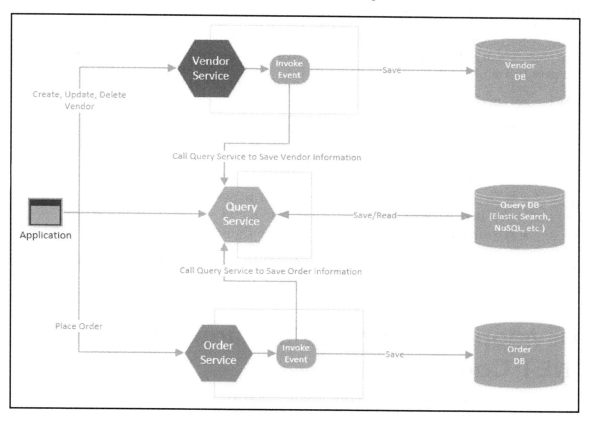

The preceding diagram represents three services: vendor service, order service, and query service. When any create, update, or delete operation is performed on the vendor service, the event is raised and the corresponding handler is invoked that makes the HTTP POST, PUT, or DELETE request on the query service to save or update its data store. The same goes for the order service, which calls the query service and stores the information related to orders. Finally, the query service is used to read the cumulative data of independent services in a single call.

The benefits of this approach are as follows:

- We can make optimize the query database by defining cluster and non-cluster indexes
- We can use some other database model, such as NoSQL, MongoDB, or Elasticsearch, to provide a faster retrieval and search experience to the user
- Each service has its own data store but, with this approach, we can aggregate the data in one place
- We can use the query data for reporting purposes

CQRS can be implemented using the mediator pattern, which we will discuss later in the chapter.

Developing microservices architecture with .NET Core

So far, we have learned the fundamentals of microservices and the importance of DDD. In this section, we will develop a microservices architecture for a sample application that contains the following features:

- Identity service
- Vendor service

Creating a sample app in .NET Core using microservices architecture

In this section, we will create a sample app in .NET Core and define services that include the authorization server, a vendor service, and an order service. To start with, we can use either Visual Studio 2017 or Visual Studio Code and create projects using dotnet **Command-Line Interface (CLI)** tools. The advantage of choosing Visual Studio 2017 is that it provides an option while creating the project to enable Docker support, add the Docker-related files, and make Docker the startup project:

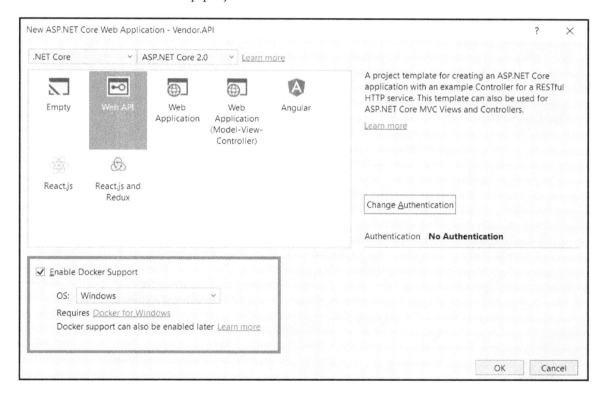

Solution structure

The structure of the solution will look like the following:

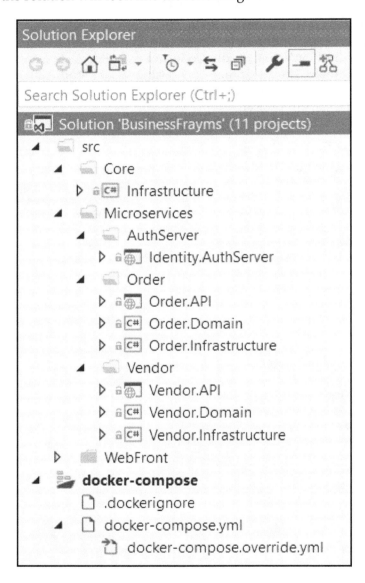

In the preceding structure, we have root folders, namely `Core`, `Microservices`, and `WebFront`. The common and core components reside in `Core`, all the microservices reside in the `Microservices` folder, and `WebFront` contains the frontend projects, most likely the ASP.NET MVC Core project, mobile application, and so on.

Creating projects inside designated folders gives proper meaning to the solution and makes it easy to understand the overall picture of the solution.

The following table shows the projects created inside each folder:

Folder	Project name	Project type	Description
Core	Infrastructure	.NET Standard 2.0	Contains repository classes, `UnitOfWork` and `BaseEntity`
Core	APIComponents	.NET Standard 2.0	Contains `BaseController`, `LoggingActionFilter` and `ResilientHttpClient`
Microservices > AuthServer	Identity.AuthServer	ASP.NET Core 2.0 web API	Authorization server using OpenIddict and ASP.NET Core Identity
Microservices > Vendor	Vendor.API	ASP.NET Core 2.0 web API	Contains vendor API controllers
Microservices > Vendor	Vendor.Domain	.NET Standard 2.0	Contains domain models specific to the vendor domain
Microservices > Vendor	Vendor.Infrastructure	.NET Standard 2.0	Contains vendor-specific repository and database context
WebFront	FraymsWebApp	ASP.NET Core 2.0 web app	Contains frontend views, pages, and client-side framework

Logical architecture

The logical architecture of the sample application represents two microservices, namely the identity service and vendor service. The identity service is used to perform user authentication and authorization, whereas the vendor service is used to perform vendor registration:

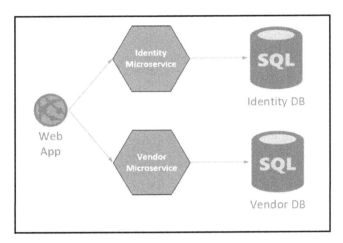

We will be using the DDD approach to articulate the data model, where each service will have its own corresponding tables.

The vendor service is based on business domain and is divided into three layers, namely the API that exposes HTTP endpoints and is used by the client, the domain that contains domain entities, aggregates, and DDD patterns, and the infrastructure layer that contains all common classes that include repository, **Entity Framework** (**EF**), Core context, and other helper classes.

The domain layer is the actual layer that defines the business logic and the entities, usually **Plain Old CLR Object** (**POCO**), for a particular business scenario. It should not have any direct dependency on any database framework or **Object Relationship Mapping** (**ORM**) such as EF, Hibernate, and others. However, with EF Core, we have a provision to keep entities separate from other assemblies and define them as POCO entities, removing dependencies from EF Core libraries.

When a request comes to an API, it uses the domain layer to execute a particular business scenario and pass the data it receives. The domain layer executes the business logic and uses the infrastructure layer to perform CRUD on the database. Finally, the response is sent back to the caller from an API:

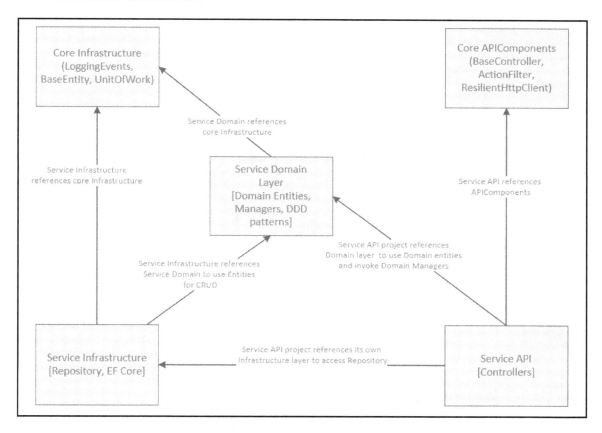

Developing a Core infrastructure project

This project contains the core classes and components used by the application. It will contain some generic or base classes, façade, and other helper classes that are common throughout the application.

We will create the following classes and discuss how they are useful for other projects specific to microservices.

Creating the BaseEntity class

The `BaseEntity` class contains common properties being used by all the domain models in our microservices projects. Usually, for all the transaction tables, we store `CreatedBy`, `CreatedOn`, `UpdatedBy`, and `UpdatedOn` fields. When designing the entity model for each service, we will inherit from the `BaseEntity` class so all these common properties will be added to the table when the migration is run. Here is the code snippet of the `BaseEntity` class:

```
public abstract class BaseEntity
{

  public BaseEntity()
  {
    this.CreatedOn = DateTime.Now;
    this.UpdatedOn = DateTime.Now;
    this.State = (int)EntityState.New;

  }
  public string CreatedBy { get; set; }
  public DateTime CreatedOn { get; set; }
  public string UpdatedBy { get; set; }
  public DateTime UpdatedOn { get; set; }
}
```

 Any property being annotated with the `NotMapped` attribute does not create corresponding fields in the backend database.

The UnitOfWork pattern

We will implement the `UnitOfWork` pattern to save the context changes in a single call to the backend database. Updating the database on each object state change is not good practice and reduces the application performance. Consider an example of a form that contains a table where each row is editable. Committing a change in a database on each row update reduces application performance. The better way is to keep each row state in memory and update the database once the form is posted. With the Unit of Work pattern, we can define an interface that contains the following four methods:

```
public interface IUnitOfWork: IDisposable
{
  void BeginTransaction();

  void RollbackTransaction();
```

```
    void CommitTransaction();

    Task<bool> SaveChangesAsync();
}
```

The interface contains transaction-related methods, namely `BeginTransaction`, `RollbackTransaction`, and `CommitTransaction`, where `SaveChangesAsync` is used to save the changes to the database. Each service has its own database context implementation and implements the `IUnitOfWork` interface to provide transaction handling and save changes to a backend database.

Creating a repository interface

We will create a generic repository interface that will be implemented by each service's repository class, as each service will be following a DDD approach and has its own repository to give meaningful information to the developer based on the business domain. In this interface, we can keep generic methods such as `All` and `Contains` and a property to return `UnitOfWork`:

```
public interface IRepository<T> where T : BaseEntity
{
    IUnitOfWork UnitOfWork { get; }

    IQueryable<T> All<T>() where T : BaseEntity;
    T Find<T>(Expression<Func<T, bool>> predicate) where T : BaseEntity;
    bool Contains<T>(Expression<Func<T, bool>> predicate) where T :
BaseEntity;
}
```

Logging

Logging is an essential part of any enterprise application. Through logging, we can trace or troubleshoot actual errors when the application is running. In any good product, we usually see that each error has an error code. Defining error codes and then using them while logging exceptions intuitively tells the developers or the support team to troubleshoot and reach the point where the actual error occurred and provide a solution. For all application-level errors, we can create a `LoggingEvents` class and specify the constant values that can be further used during development. Here is the `LoggingEvents` class that contains a few GET, CREATE, UPDATE, and other event codes. We can create this class under a `Façade` folder inside the `Infrastructure` project:

```
public static class LoggingEvents
{
```

```
    public const int GET_ITEM = 1001;
    public const int GET_ITEMS = 1002;
    public const int CREATE_ITEM = 1003;
    public const int UPDATE_ITEM = 1004;
    public const int DELETE_ITEM = 1005;
    public const int DATABASE_ERROR = 2000;
    public const int SERVICE_ERROR = 2001;
    public const int ERROR = 2002;
    public const int ACCESS_METHOD = 3000;
}
```

Next, we will add another class, `LoggerHelper`, which will be used throughout our application to get the exception stack trace from the exception. Here is the code snippet of the `LoggerHelper` class:

```
public static string GetExceptionDetails(Exception ex)
{

  StringBuilder errorString = new StringBuilder();
  errorString.AppendLine("An error occured. ");
  Exception inner = ex;
  while (inner != null)
  {
    errorString.Append("Error Message:");
    errorString.AppendLine(ex.Message);
    errorString.Append("Stack Trace:");
    errorString.AppendLine(ex.StackTrace);
    inner = inner.InnerException;
  }
  return errorString.ToString();
}
```

Creating the APIComponents infrastructure project

The APIComponents project contains the components specific to microservices. In this project, we will create a `BaseController` class, which will add some classes related to logging and can also extend to add further common objects used by concrete controllers. Add a `BaseController` class under the `Controllers` folder inside the `APIComponents` project. Here is the code snippet of the `BaseController` class:

```
public class BaseController : Controller
{
  private ILogger _logger;
  public BaseController(ILogger logger)
  {
    _logger = logger;
```

```
  }

  public ILogger Logger { get { return _logger; } }
  public HttpResponseMessage LogException(Exception ex)
  {
    HttpResponseMessage message = new HttpResponseMessage();
    message.Content = new StringContent(ex.Message);
    message.StatusCode = System.Net.HttpStatusCode.ExpectationFailed;
    return message;
  }
}
```

BaseController takes ILogger in a parametrized constructor that will be injected through the built-in **Dependency Injection** (**DI**) component of ASP.NET Core.

The LogException method is used to log the exception and returns the HttpResponseMessage that will be returned by the derived controller to the user in case of any error.

Next, we will add the Filters folder inside the APIComponents project and add all the common filters that can be used by the microservices controllers. For now, we will just add the LoggingActionFilter that can be used by annotating the Action methods of the microservices controllers and automatically logging the information when the request comes in and response goes out. Here is the code snippet of the LoggingActionFilter class:

```
public class LoggingActionFilter: ActionFilterAttribute
{
  public override void OnActionExecuting(ActionExecutingContext context)
  {

    Log("OnActionExecuting", context.RouteData, context.Controller);

  }

  public override void OnActionExecuted(ActionExecutedContext context)
  {
    Log("OnActionExecuted", context.RouteData, context.Controller);

  }

  public override void OnResultExecuted(ResultExecutedContext context)
  {
    Log("OnResultExecuted", context.RouteData, context.Controller);
  }
```

```
public override void OnResultExecuting(ResultExecutingContext context)
{
  Log("OnResultExecuting", context.RouteData, context.Controller);
}

private void Log(string methodName, RouteData routeData, Object
controller)
{
  var controllerName = routeData.Values["controller"];
  var actionName = routeData.Values["action"];
  var message = String.Format("{0} controller:{1} action:{2}",
  methodName, controllerName, actionName);
  BaseController baseController = ((BaseController)controller);
  baseController.Logger.LogInformation(LoggingEvents.ACCESS_METHOD,
message);
  }
}
```

In this project, we also have `ResilientHttpClient` that we learned in `Chapter 7`, *Securing and Implementing Resilience in .NET Core Applications*.

Developing an identity service for user authorization

In ASP.NET Core, we have a choice of authenticating applications from various authentication providers. In microservices architecture, services are deployed and hosted separately in different containers. We can use ASP.NET Core Identity and add it as middleware in the service itself, or we can use IdentityServer and develop a central authentication server to perform authentication and authorization centrally, access all the services that are registered with the **Central Authentication Server** (**CAS**), and access protected resources by passing tokens.

The identity service basically acts as a CAS that registers all the services in the enterprise. When the request comes to the service, it asks for the token that can be obtained from the authorization server. Once the token is obtained, it can be used to access the resource service.

There are various libraries to build the authentication server, which are as follows:

- **IdentityServer4**: IdentityServer4 is an OpenID Connect and OAuth 2.0 framework for ASP.NET Core
- **OpenIddict**: Easy to plug in solution to implement OpenID Connect server in ASP.NET Core project

- **ASOS (AspNet.Security.OpenIdConnect.Server)**: ASOS is an advanced OpenID Connect server designed to offer a low-level protocol-first approach

We will be using OpenIddict in our identity service.

OpenIddict connect flows

OpenIddict offers various types of flows, including authorization code flow, password flow, client credentials flow, and others. However, we have used implicit flow in this chapter.

In implicit flow, the tokens are retrieved through the authorization endpoint by passing a username and password. All communication is done with the authorization server in a single round trip. Once the authentication is done, the token is added in the redirect URI and can be later used by passing in the request header for subsequent requests. The following diagram depicts how implicit flow works:

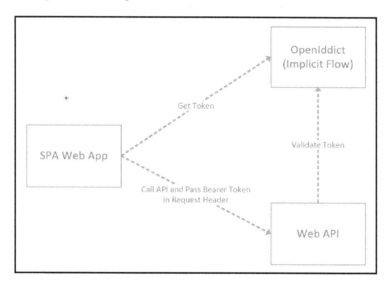

Implicit flow is widely used with **Single-Page Applications (SPAs)**. The process starts when an SPA web application wants to access the protected web API from the resource server. As the web API is protected, it needs a token to authenticate the request and validate the caller. To obtain the token (commonly known as a bearer token), the SPA web app first proceeds to the authorization server and enters the username and password. After successful authentication, the authorization server returns the token and appends it to the redirect URI itself. The web application parses the **Uniform Resource Locator (URL)** and retrieves the token and further used to access the protected resources.

Creating the identity service project

The identity service is an ASP.NET Core web API project. To use OpenIddict libraries, we have to add an `aspnet-contrib` reference to our Visual Studio package sources dialog. To add this source from Visual Studio, click on the NuGet Package Manager by right-clicking on the project and then hitting the settings button, as shown in the following screenshot:

Then add the entry of `aspnet-contrib` with the source as `https://www.myget.org/F/aspnet-contrib/api/v3/index.json`:

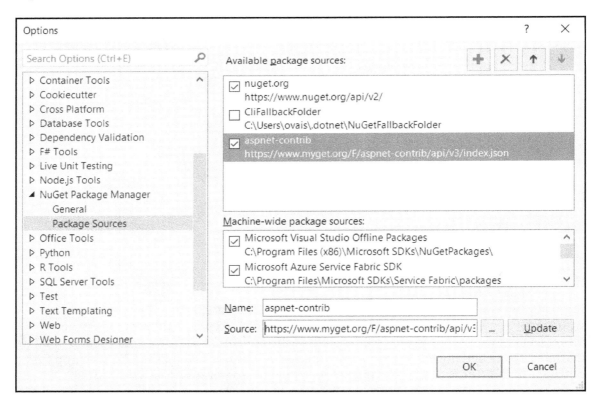

Once this is added, we can now easily add OpenIddict packages from the NuGet Package Manager window.

Remember to check that the **Include prerelease** checkbox is selected.

The following are the packages that we can add directly to our project file or from the NuGet Package Manager window in Visual Studio:

```
<PackageReference Include="AspNet.Security.OAuth.Validation"
Version="2.0.0-rc1-final" />
<PackageReference Include="AspNet.Security.OpenIdConnect.Server"
Version="2.0.0-rc1-final" />
<PackageReference Include="Microsoft.AspNetCore.Identity" Version="2.0.1"
/>
<PackageReference
Include="Microsoft.AspNetCore.Identity.EntityFrameworkCore" Version="2.0.1"
/>
<PackageReference
Include="Microsoft.VisualStudio.Web.CodeGeneration.Design" Version="2.0.2"
/>
<PackageReference Include="OpenIddict" Version="2.0.0-rc2-0797" />
<PackageReference Include="OpenIddict.Core" Version="2.0.0-rc2-0797" />
<PackageReference Include="OpenIddict.EntityFrameworkCore" Version="2.0.0-
rc2-0797" />
<PackageReference Include="OpenIddict.Models" Version="2.0.0-rc2-0797" />
<PackageReference Include="OpenIddict.Mvc" Version="2.0.0-rc2-0797" />
```

Add custom UserEntity and UserRole classes

ASP.NET Core Identity contains `IdentityUser` and `IdentityRole` classes and uses EF Core to create a backend database. However, if we want to customize the default tables, we can do so by inheriting from these base classes.

We will create a `Models` folder and customize `IdentityUser` by creating a custom `UserEntity` class and adding the following four fields:

```
public class UserEntity : IdentityUser<Guid>
{

  public int VendorId { get; set; }

  public string FirstName { get; set; }
  public string LastName { get; set; }

  public DateTimeOffset CreatedAt { get; set; }
}
```

We have added these fields so when a vendor registers, we will keep their first name, last name, and ID in this table. Next, we add another class, `UserRole`, which derives from `IdentityRole`, and add the parametrized constructor as follows:

```
public class UserRoleEntity : IdentityRole<Guid>
{
  public UserRoleEntity() : base() { }

  public UserRoleEntity(string roleName) : base(roleName) { }
}
```

We will add the custom database context class that derives from `IdentityDbContext` and specify `UserEntity` and `UserRoleEntity` types as follows:

```
public class BFIdentityContext : IdentityDbContext<UserEntity,
UserRoleEntity, Guid>
{
  public BFIdentityContext(Microsoft.EntityFrameworkCore.DbContextOptions
options) :
  base(options) { }
}
```

We can run EF Core migrations to create ASP.NET Identity tables, and we can run migration using EF CLI tooling. Before running the migration, we add the following entries in the `ConfigureServices` method of our `Startup` class:

```
public void ConfigureServices(IServiceCollection services)
{
  var connection= Configuration["ConnectionString"];

  services.AddDbContext<BFIdentityContext>(options =>
  {
    // Configure the context to use Microsoft SQL Server.
    options.UseSqlServer(connection);
  });

  services.AddIdentity<UserEntity,
UserRole>().AddEntityFrameworkStores<BFIdentityContext>();

  services.AddMvc();
}
```

You can run the EF migrations from the Visual Studio Package Manager Console window. To add migration, first run the following command:

```
Add-Migration Initial
```

Add-Migration is the command of EF CLI toolset, where Initial is the name of the migration. Once we run this command, it will add the Migrations folder into our project and the Initial class containing Up and Down methods to apply or remove changes to the database. Next, we can run the Update-Database command that loads the Initial class and apply the changes to the backend database.

Now we add the configuration related to the OpenIddict implicit flow in our Startup class. Here is the modified ConfigureServices method that adds the OpenIddict implicit flow:

```
public void ConfigureServices(IServiceCollection services)
{
    var connection = @"Server=.sqlexpress;Database=FraymsIdentityDB;
    User Id=sa;Password=P@ssw0rd;";

    services.AddDbContext<BFIdentityContext>(options =>
    {
        // Configure the context to use Microsoft SQL Server.
        options.UseSqlServer(connection);

        // Register the entity sets needed by OpenIddict.
        // Note: use the generic overload if you need
        // to replace the default OpenIddict entities.
        options.UseOpenIddict();
    });

    services.AddIdentity<UserEntity, UserRoleEntity>()
    .AddEntityFrameworkStores<BFIdentityContext>();

    // Configure Identity to use the same JWT claims as OpenIddict instead
    // of the legacy WS-Federation claims it uses by default (ClaimTypes),
    // which saves you from doing the mapping in your authorization
controller.
    services.Configure<IdentityOptions>(options =>
    {
        options.ClaimsIdentity.UserNameClaimType =
OpenIdConnectConstants.Claims.Name;
        options.ClaimsIdentity.UserIdClaimType =
OpenIdConnectConstants.Claims.Subject;
        options.ClaimsIdentity.RoleClaimType =
OpenIdConnectConstants.Claims.Role;
    });

    // Register the OpenIddict services.
    services.AddOpenIddict(options =>
    {
        // Register the Entity Framework stores.
```

```
        options.AddEntityFrameworkCoreStores<BFIdentityContext>();

        // Register the ASP.NET Core MVC binder used by OpenIddict.
        // Note: if you don't call this method, you won't be able to
        // bind OpenIdConnectRequest or OpenIdConnectResponse parameters.
        options.AddMvcBinders();

        // Enable the authorization, logout, userinfo, and introspection
    endpoints.
        options.EnableAuthorizationEndpoint("/connect/authorize")
        .EnableLogoutEndpoint("/connect/logout")
        .EnableIntrospectionEndpoint("/connect/introspect")
        .EnableUserinfoEndpoint("/api/userinfo");

        // Note: the sample only uses the implicit code flow but you can enable
        // the other flows if you need to support implicit, password or client
    credentials.
        options.AllowImplicitFlow();
        // During development, you can disable the HTTPS requirement.
        options.DisableHttpsRequirement();

        // Register a new ephemeral key, that is discarded when the application
        // shuts down. Tokens signed using this key are automatically
    invalidated.
        // This method should only be used during development.
        options.AddEphemeralSigningKey();

        options.UseJsonWebTokens();
    });

    services.AddAuthentication()
    .AddOAuthValidation();

    services.AddCors();
    services.AddMvc();
}
```

In the preceding method, we first add the `UseOpenIddict` method in the `AddDbContext` options that will create the OpenIddict-related tables in the database. Then, we configure Identity to use the same **JSON Web Tokens (JWT)** claims as OpenIddict by setting the `IdentityOptions` as follows:

```
services.Configure<IdentityOptions>(options =>
{
    options.ClaimsIdentity.UserNameClaimType =
OpenIdConnectConstants.Claims.Name;
```

```
  options.ClaimsIdentity.UserIdClaimType =
OpenIdConnectConstants.Claims.Subject;
  options.ClaimsIdentity.RoleClaimType =
OpenIdConnectConstants.Claims.Role;
});
```

Finally, we register the OpenIddict features and specify values by calling the `services.AddOpenIddict` method.

Here is the `Configure` method that first enables **Cross-Origin Resource Sharing** (**CORS**), which allows requests from any header, origin, and method. Then, add authentication and call the `InitializeAsync` method to populate the OpenIddict tables with the application and resources (services) information:

```
public void Configure(IApplicationBuilder app)
{
  app.UseCors(builder =>
  {
    builder.AllowAnyOrigin();
    builder.AllowAnyHeader();
    builder.AllowAnyMethod();
  });

  app.UseAuthentication();

  app.UseMvcWithDefaultRoute();

  // Seed the database with the sample applications.
  // Note: in a real world application, this step should be part of a setup
script.
  InitializeAsync(app.ApplicationServices,
CancellationToken.None).GetAwaiter().GetResult();
}
```

Here is the `InitializeAsync` method shown as follows:

```
private async Task InitializeAsync(IServiceProvider services,
CancellationToken cancellationToken)
{
  // Create a new service scope to ensure the database context
  // is correctly disposed when this methods returns.
  using (var scope =
services.GetRequiredService<IServiceScopeFactory>().CreateScope())
  {
    var context =
scope.ServiceProvider.GetRequiredService<BFIdentityContext>();
    await context.Database.EnsureCreatedAsync();
```

```
    var manager = scope.ServiceProvider.GetRequiredService
    <OpenIddictApplicationManager<OpenIddictApplication>>();

    if (await manager.FindByClientIdAsync("bfrwebapp", cancellationToken)
== null)
    {
      var descriptor = new OpenIddictApplicationDescriptor
      {
        ClientId = "bfrwebapp",
        DisplayName = "Business Frayms web application",
        PostLogoutRedirectUris = { new
Uri("http://localhost:8080/signout-oidc") },
        RedirectUris = { new Uri("http://localhost:8080/signin-oidc") }
      };

      await manager.CreateAsync(descriptor, cancellationToken);
    }

    if (await manager.FindByClientIdAsync("vendor-api", cancellationToken)
== null)
    {
      var descriptor = new OpenIddictApplicationDescriptor
      {
        ClientId = "vendor-api",
        ClientSecret = "846B62D0-DEF9-4215-A99D-86E6B8DAB342",
        //RedirectUris = { new Uri("http://localhost:12345/api") }
      };

      await manager.CreateAsync(descriptor, cancellationToken);
    }

  }
}
```

In the preceding method, we have added the following three applications:

- bfrwebapp: An ASP.NET Core web application. When the user hits the web application, it checks whether the user is authenticated based on whether the token is provided. If the user is not authenticated, it will redirect it to the authorization server. The user enters the credentials and, with successful authentication, it will redirect back to the bfrwebapp. The redirect URI specified within this scope is the URI of bfrwebapp.
- vendor-api: A vendor microservice with a unique client secret key.

The preceding configuration is the server-side configuration and we will see what configuration needs to be added on the client side.

Finally, we will add `AuthorizationController` under the `Controllers` folder to implement endpoints defined for the authorization server in the `ConfigureServices` method in the `Startup` class. Here is the complete code snippet of the `AuthorizationController`:

```
public class AuthorizationController : Controller
{
  private readonly IOptions<IdentityOptions> _identityOptions;
  private readonly SignInManager<UserEntity> _signInManager;
  private readonly UserManager<UserEntity> _userManager;

  public AuthorizationController(
    IOptions<IdentityOptions> identityOptions,
    SignInManager<UserEntity> signInManager,
    UserManager<UserEntity> userManager)
  {
    _identityOptions = identityOptions;
    _signInManager = signInManager;
    _userManager = userManager;
  }

  [HttpGet("~/connect/authorize")]
  public async Task<IActionResult> Authorize(OpenIdConnectRequest request)
  {
    Debug.Assert(request.IsAuthorizationRequest(),
    "The OpenIddict binder for ASP.NET Core MVC is not registered. " +
    "Make sure services.AddOpenIddict().AddMvcBinders() is correctly
called.");

    if (!User.Identity.IsAuthenticated)
    {
      // If the client application request promptless authentication,
      // return an error indicating that the user is not logged in.
      if (request.HasPrompt(OpenIdConnectConstants.Prompts.None))
      {
        var properties = new AuthenticationProperties(new
Dictionary<string, string>
        {
          [OpenIdConnectConstants.Properties.Error] =
          OpenIdConnectConstants.Errors.LoginRequired,
          [OpenIdConnectConstants.Properties.ErrorDescription] =
          "The user is not logged in."
        });

        // Ask OpenIddict to return a login_required error to the client
application.
        return Forbid(properties,
```

```
OpenIdConnectServerDefaults.AuthenticationScheme);
    }

    return Challenge();
  }

  // Retrieve the profile of the logged in user.
  var user = await _userManager.GetUserAsync(User);
  if (user == null)
  {
    return BadRequest(new OpenIdConnectResponse
    {
      Error = OpenIdConnectConstants.Errors.InvalidGrant,
      ErrorDescription = "The username/password couple is invalid."
    });
  }

  // Create a new authentication ticket.
  var ticket = await CreateTicketAsync(request, user);

  // Returning a SignInResult will ask OpenIddict to issue
  the appropriate access/identity tokens.
  return SignIn(ticket.Principal, ticket.Properties,
ticket.AuthenticationScheme);
  }

  [HttpGet("~/connect/logout")]
  public async Task<IActionResult> Logout()
  {
    // Ask ASP.NET Core Identity to delete the local and external cookies
created
    // when the user agent is redirected from the external identity
provider
    // after a successful authentication flow (e.g Google or Facebook).
    await _signInManager.SignOutAsync();

    // Returning a SignOutResult will ask OpenIddict to redirect the user
agent
    // to the post_logout_redirect_uri specified by the client application.
    return SignOut(OpenIdConnectServerDefaults.AuthenticationScheme);
  }

  private async Task<AuthenticationTicket> CreateTicketAsync(
  OpenIdConnectRequest request, UserEntity user)
  {
    // Create a new ClaimsPrincipal containing the claims that
    // will be used to create an id_token, a token or a code.
    var principal = await _signInManager.CreateUserPrincipalAsync(user);
```

```
// Create a new authentication ticket holding the user identity.
var ticket = new AuthenticationTicket(principal,
new AuthenticationProperties(),
OpenIdConnectServerDefaults.AuthenticationScheme);

// Set the list of scopes granted to the client application.
ticket.SetScopes(new[]
{
  OpenIdConnectConstants.Scopes.OpenId,
  OpenIdConnectConstants.Scopes.Email,
  OpenIdConnectConstants.Scopes.Profile,
  OpenIddictConstants.Scopes.Roles
}.Intersect(request.GetScopes()));

ticket.SetResources("vendor-api");

// Note: by default, claims are NOT automatically included in
// the access and identity tokens.
// To allow OpenIddict to serialize them, you must attach them a
destination, that specifies
// whether they should be included in access tokens, in identity tokens
or in both.

foreach (var claim in ticket.Principal.Claims)
{
  // Never include the security stamp in the access and
  // identity tokens, as it's a secret value.
  if (claim.Type ==
_identityOptions.Value.ClaimsIdentity.SecurityStampClaimType)
  {
    continue;
  }

  var destinations = new List<string>
  {
    OpenIdConnectConstants.Destinations.AccessToken
  };

  // Only add the iterated claim to the id_token if
  // the corresponding scope was granted to the client application.
  // The other claims will only be added to the access_token,
  // which is encrypted when using the default format.
  if ((claim.Type == OpenIdConnectConstants.Claims.Name &&
  ticket.HasScope(OpenIdConnectConstants.Scopes.Profile)) ||
  (claim.Type == OpenIdConnectConstants.Claims.Email &&
  ticket.HasScope(OpenIdConnectConstants.Scopes.Email)) ||
  (claim.Type == OpenIdConnectConstants.Claims.Role &&
  ticket.HasScope(OpenIddictConstants.Claims.Roles)))
```

```
        {
destinations.Add(OpenIdConnectConstants.Destinations.IdentityToken);
        }

    claim.SetDestinations(destinations);
    }

    return ticket;
    }
}
```

`AuthorizationController` exposes two methods, namely `authorize` and `logout`. The `authorize` method checks whether the user is authenticated and returns a challenge that shows the login page, where the user can enter their username and password. Once the correct credentials are entered and the user is validated from the identity tables, the authorization server creates a new authentication token and returns it to the client application based on the redirect URI specified for `bfrwebapp`. To see the working example, please refer to the code repository.

Implementing the vendor service

The vendor service is a web API that exposes a method to perform vendor registration. This service implements the actual business domain of the vendor system where a vendor can register. As we learned in the previous section, we can decompose an application based on business capability or business domain. This service implements a DDD principle and decomposes based on business domain. It contains the following three projects:

- `Vendor.API`: An ASP.NET Core Web API project that exposes methods to register a vendor
- `Vendor.Domain`: .NET Standard 2.0 class library that contains POCO models such as `VendorMaster` and `VendorDocument`, and an `IVendorRepository` interface to define methods essential for a vendor domain.
- `Vendor.Infrastructure`: .NET Standard 2.0 class library that contains a `VendorRepository` that implements the `IVendorRepository` interface and a `VendorDBContext` to perform database operations.

Creating a vendor domain

Create a new .NET Standard library project and name it `Vendor.Domain`. We will reference our `Infrastructure` project created previously to derive our POCO entities from the `BaseEntity` class.

Create a `VendorMaster` class and derive it from the `BaseEntity` class. Here is the code snippet of `VendorMaster` class:

```
public class VendorMaster : BaseEntity
{
  [Key]
  public int ID { get; set; }
  public string VendorName { get; set; }
  public string ContractNumber { get; set; }
  public string Email { get; set; }
  public string Title { get; set; }
  public string PrimaryContactPersonName{ get; set; }
  public string PrimaryContactEmail { get; set; }
  public string PrimaryContactNumber { get; set; }
  public string SecondaryContactPersonName { get; set; }
  public string SecondaryContactEmail { get; set; }
  public string SecondaryContactNumber { get; set; }
  public string Website { get; set; }
  public string FaxNumber { get; set; }
  public string AddressLine1 { get; set; }
  public string AddressLine2 { get; set; }
  public string City { get; set; }
  public string State { get; set; }
  public string Country { get; set; }

  public List<VendorDocument> VendorDocuments { get; set; }

}
```

`VendorDocument` is another POCO class that contains document-related fields. Here is the code snippet of the `VendorDocument` class:

```
public class VendorDocument : BaseEntity
{

  [Key]
  public int ID { get; set; }
  public string DocumentName { get; set; }
  public string DocumentType { get; set; }
  public Byte[] DocumentContent { get; set; }
  public DateTime DocumentExpiry { get; set; }

  public int VendorMasterID { get; set; }

  [ForeignKey("VendorMasterID")]
  public VendorMaster VendorMaster { get; set; }
```

```
}
```

Next, we will add the `IVendorRepository` interface to expose methods specific to the vendor domain. Here is the code snippet of the `IVendorRepository` interface:

```
public interface IVendorRepository : IRepository<VendorMaster>
{
  VendorMaster Add(VendorMaster vendorMaster);

  void Update(VendorMaster vendorMaster);

  Task<VendorMaster> GetAsync(int vendorID);

  void Add(VendorDocument vendorDocument);

  void Delete(int vendorDocumentID);
}
```

Creating the vendor infrastructure

This project is a .NET Standard 2.0 class library project that reference the core `Infrastructure` and `Vendor.Domain` projects. This contains the actual implementation of the `VendorRepository` and a database context to connect with the backend SQL Server database.

Here is the `VendorDBContext` class that derives from the `DbContext` class of EF Core and defines `DbSet` for the `VendorMaster` and `VendorDocument` entities:

```
public class VendorDBContext : DbContext, IUnitOfWork
{

  public VendorDBContext(DbContextOptions options) : base(options)
  {

  }

  protected override void OnConfiguring(DbContextOptionsBuilder
optionsBuilder)
  {
    base.OnConfiguring(optionsBuilder);
    // optionsBuilder.UseSqlServer(@"Data Source=.sqlexpress;
    Initial Catalog=FraymsVendorDB;Integrated Security=False; User Id=sa;
    Password=P@ssw0rd; Timeout=500000;");
  }
```

```
protected override void OnModelCreating(ModelBuilder builder)
{
  base.OnModelCreating(builder);
}

public void BeginTransaction()
{
  this.Database.BeginTransaction();
}
public void RollbackTransaction()
{
  this.Database.RollbackTransaction();
}
public void CommitTransaction()
{
  this.Database.CommitTransaction();
}
public Task<bool> SaveChangesAsync()
{
  return this.SaveChangesAsync();
}

public DbSet<VendorMaster> VendorMaster { get; set; }
public DbSet<VendorDocument> VendorDocuments { get; protected set; }
```

We will also implement the `IUnitOfWork` interface, so when the `VendorRepository` is injected in a controller, we can perform transaction handling and save the changes to the associated database in a single call.

Here is the `VendorRepository` that implements the `IVendorRepository` interface:

```
public class VendorRepository : IVendorRepository
{

  VendorDBContext _dbContext;


  public VendorRepository(VendorDBContext dbContext)
  {
    this._dbContext = dbContext;
  }
  public IUnitOfWork UnitOfWork
  {
    get
    {
      return _dbContext;
    }
```

```
  }

  public VendorMaster Add(VendorMaster vendorMaster)
  {
    var res= _dbContext.Add(vendorMaster);
    return res.Entity;
  }
  public void AddDocument(VendorDocument vendorDocument)
  {
    var res = _dbContext.Add(vendorDocument);
  }

  public void Update(VendorMaster vendorMaster)
  {
    _dbContext.Entry(vendorMaster).State =
Microsoft.EntityFrameworkCore.EntityState.Modified;
  }

  public async Task<VendorMaster> GetAsync(int vendorID)
  {
    var vendorMaster = await _dbContext.VendorMaster.FindAsync(vendorID);
    if (vendorMaster != null)
    {
      await _dbContext.Entry(vendorMaster)
      .Collection(i => i.VendorDocuments).LoadAsync();
    }
    return vendorMaster;
  }


  public IQueryable<T> All<T>() where T : BaseEntity
  {
    return _dbContext.Set<T>().AsQueryable();
  }

  public bool Contains<T>(Expression<Func<T, bool>> predicate) where T :
BaseEntity
  {
    return _dbContext.Set<T>().Count<T>(predicate) > 0;
  }

  public T Find<T>(Expression<Func<T, bool>> predicate) where T :
BaseEntity
  {
    return _dbContext.Set<T>().FirstOrDefault<T>(predicate);
  }
}
```

Creating the vendor service

We will now create a vendor-service project that will expose methods for use by client applications to register a vendor. To start with, let's create a new ASP.NET Core web API project and name it `Vendor.API`.

Implementing the mediator pattern in the vendor service

In microservices architecture, an application is split into multiple services, where each service connects to the other services through an endpoint. There are possibilities that one service may invoke or interact with multiple services when the event is invoked. Segregating the interaction between services is always a recommended approach and solves tight dependencies on other services. For example, an application invokes this service to register a vendor and then invoke the identity service to create its user account and send an email by calling the messaging service. We can implement the mediator pattern to solve this scenario.

The mediator pattern is based on the event-driven topology that works as a publisher/subscriber model. When any event is invoked, the registered handlers are called and execute the underlying logic. This encapsulates the logic of how services interact with one another, keeping the actual logic separate for each interaction. Moreover, the code is clean and easy to change.

In `Vendor.API`, we will implement the mediator pattern using the `MediatR` library of .NET. `MediatR` is the implementation of the mediator pattern that supports command handling and domain event publishing. In the following section, we will implement mediator when the user registers and invoke the identity service to create a new user and send an email.

To use `MediatR`, we have to add the following two packages:

- `MediatR`
- `MediatR.Extensions.Microsoft.DependencyInjection`

After adding these packages, we can add it in the `ConfigureServices` method by calling the `services.AddMediatR` method. `MediatR` provides the following two types of messages:

- **Request/response**: Requests are commands that may or may not return a value
- **Notification**: Notifications are events that may not return a value

In our example, we will implement both request/response to save a vendor record into a database and, once it returns Boolean true as a response, we will invoke notification events to create a vendor user and send an email.

To implement request/response, we should define a class that implements the interface of `IRequestHandler`or `IRequestHandlet<TRequest, TResponse>`, where `TRequest` is the request object type and `TResponse` is the response object type.

Create a class `CreateVendorCommand` under the `Commands` folder in your `Vendor.API` project. Here is the code snippet of `CreateVendorCommand`:

```
public class CreateVendorCommand : IRequest<bool>
{

  [DataMember]
  public VendorViewModel VendorViewModel { get; set; }

  public CreateVendorCommand(VendorViewModel vendorViewModel)
  {
    VendorViewModel = vendorViewModel;
  }

}
```

It implements the `IRequest` class that returns a Boolean value as a response. We have also specified our `VendorViewModel` that will be injected by the `MediatR` library when we pass them while calling the `send` method in the `VendorController` class.

Next, we will create a command handler that implements the generic `IRequestHandler<TRequest, TResponse>`, where `TRequest` is the `CreateVendorCommand` and `TResponse` will be a Boolean type. Here is the code snippet of `CreateVendorCommandHandler`:

```
public class CreateVendorCommandHandler :
IRequestHandler<CreateVendorCommand, bool>
{
  private readonly IVendorRepository _vendorRepository;

  public CreateVendorCommandHandler(IVendorRepository vendorRepository)
  {
    _vendorRepository = vendorRepository;
  }

  public async Task<bool> Handle(CreateVendorCommand command,
  CancellationToken cancellationToken)
```

```
{
    _vendorRepository.UnitOfWork.BeginTransaction();
    try
    {
      _vendorRepository.Add(command.VendorMaster);
      _vendorRepository.UnitOfWork.CommitTransaction();
    }catch(Exception ex)
    {
      _vendorRepository.UnitOfWork.RollbackTransaction();
    }
    return await _vendorRepository.UnitOfWork.SaveChangesAsync();
  }
}
```

When this handler is invoked, it will call the `Handle` method and pass the command and the cancellation token. From the command object, we can get the object we have passed while calling the `Send` method of the `IMediator` object in the `VendorController` class. This method calls the `Add` method of the `VendorRepository` and saves the information into the database. With the request/response approach, only one command handler is executed even if you have multiple handlers defined for the command. To call all the handlers, we can use notifications. We will extend the preceding example and add notification events and corresponding handlers that will be invoked once the command is executed successfully.

First, we define the notification event by creating a class and implementing the `INotification` interface. Here is the code snippet of the `CreateVendorNotification` event that will be used by the notification handlers:

```
public class CreateVendorNotification : INotification
{
  public VendorMaster _vendorVM;
  public CreateVendorNotification(VendorMaster vendorVM)
  {
    _vendorVM = vendorVM;
  }
}
```

Here is the implementation of `CreateUserHandler`, which listens for the `CreateVendorNotification` event to be raised. Once the event is raised, it is invoked and executes the logic defined in the `Handle` method. We use `CreateUserHandler` to create a user in the ASP.NET Core Identity database by calling the identity service. Here is the code snippet of `CreateUserHandler`:

```
public class CreateUserHandler :
```

```
INotificationHandler<CreateVendorNotification>
{
  IResilientHttpClient _client;
  public CreateUserHandler(IResilientHttpClient client)
  {
    _client = client;
  }
  public Task Handle(CreateVendorNotification notification,
CancellationToken cancellationToken)
  {
    string uri = "http://businessfrayms.com/api/Identity";
    string token = "";//read token from user session
    var response = _client.Post<VendorMaster>(uri,
notification._vendorVM,"");
    return Task.FromResult(0);
  }
}
```

Next, we will create a `SendEmailHandler` that listens for the
`CreateVendorNotification` and sends an email notification to the vendor about
registration. Here is the code snippet of `SendEmailHandler`:

```
public class SendEmailHandler :
INotificationHandler<CreateVendorNotification>
{

  MessagingService _service;
  public SendEmailHandler(MessagingService service) : base()
  {
    _service = service;
  }

  public Task Handle(CreateVendorNotification notification,
CancellationToken cancellationToken)
  {
    _service.SendEmail(notification._vendorVM.Email, "Registration",
    "Thankyou for registration");
    return Task.FromResult(0);
  }
}
```

We can add more notification handlers based on the requirements. For example, if we want
to initiate a workflow notification once the vendor record is saved into the database, we can
create a vendor workflow notification handler, and so on.

From the `VendorController` side, we can invoke the mediator pattern by calling the `Send` and `Publish` methods. The `Send` method invokes command handlers and `Publish` is used to invoke notification handlers. Here is the code snippet of `VendorController`:

```
[Produces("application/json")]
[Route("api/Vendor")]
public class VendorController : BaseController
{
  private readonly IMediator _mediator;
  private ILogger _logger;

  public VendorController(IMediator mediator, ILogger logger) :
base(logger)
    {
      _mediator = mediator;
      _logger = logger;
    }

  [Authorize(AuthenticationSchemes =
OAuthIntrospectionDefaults.AuthenticationScheme)]
  // POST: api/VendorMaster
  [HttpPost]
  public void Post([FromBody]VendorMaster value)
  {
    try
    {
      bool result = _mediator.Send(new CreateVendorCommand(value)).Result;
      if (result)
      {
        //Record saved succesfully, publishing event now
        _mediator.Publish(new CreateVendorNotification(value));
      }
    }
    catch (Exception ex)
    {
      _logger.LogError(ex.Message);
    }
  }

}
```

In the preceding code, we have a `Post` method that will be called by the client application to create a new vendor. It first calls the `Send` method, which invokes the `CreateVendorCommandHandler` and saves the record in the database, and, once the record is created and the response is true, it will invoke the `SendEmailHandler` to send an email.

 You can access the complete sample application from the GitHub link provided with the book.

Deploying microservices on Docker containers

Microservices are best suited for containerization deployment. A container is a process that provides an isolated and controlled environment for an application to run without affecting the system or vice versa. Most of us have experienced hosting applications inside VMs, which provide an isolated space to install, configure, and run applications and use the dedicated resources without affecting the underlying system or application. In contrast to VMs, containers provide the same level of isolation but are more lightweight in terms of startup time and overhead. Unlike VMs, containers do not preallocate resources such as memory, disk, and CPU usage. We can run multiple containers on the same machine, where the containers are isolated from each other but share the memory, disk, and CPU usage. This enables any application running in a container to use the maximum resources available without having any preallocated or assigned.

The following diagram depicts how VMs run on the host OS:

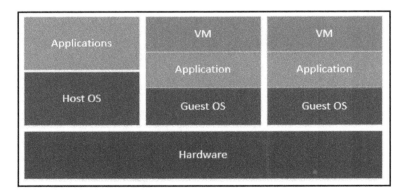

We run applications on the host OS and VMs on a guest OS. The virtualization is done at the hardware level, where VMs can talk to the host hardware using drivers available in the hypervisor virtualization system, as provided by the host OS.

Here is how containers run on the host OS:

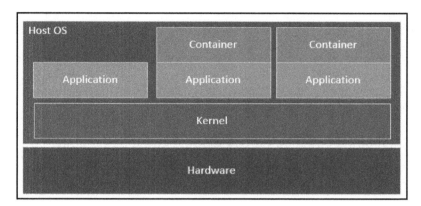

With containers, the kernel is shared between multiple containers. The kernel is a core component of the operating system that is responsible for interacting with different processes and hardware, and manages resources such as CPU cycles and virtual management. The kernel is the component that creates isolation between different containers.

What is Docker?

Docker is a software company that provides containers. Docker containers are very popular in the software industry to run microservices. They are best suited to microservices application development and provide a set of command-line tools that provide a unified way of building and maintaining different container images. We can create custom images or use existing ones from a registry such as Docker Hub (`http://hub.docker.com`).

Here are a few benefits of Docker:

Benefit	Description
Simplicity	Provides a powerful tool for application creation and orchestration
Openness	Built with open source technology and easy to integrate into existing environments

Independence	Creates separation of concerns between application and infrastructure

Using Docker with .NET Core

.NET Core is modular and faster when compared to the .NET framework and helps in running applications side by side, where each application is running its own set of CLR libraries and runtime. This makes it perfect for running on Docker containers. The image of .NET Core is far smaller when compared to the image having .NET framework installed. .NET Core uses a Windows Nano server or Linux image, which is a lot smaller than the Windows service core image. As .NET Core runs cross-platform, we can also create Docker images of other platforms and run applications on them.

With Visual Studio 2017, we can choose Docker while creating a .NET Core or ASP.NET Core project, and it auto scaffolds the Docker files and sets up the basic configuration to run applications on Docker. The following screenshot shows the Docker options available in Visual Studio 2017 to provision Docker containers:

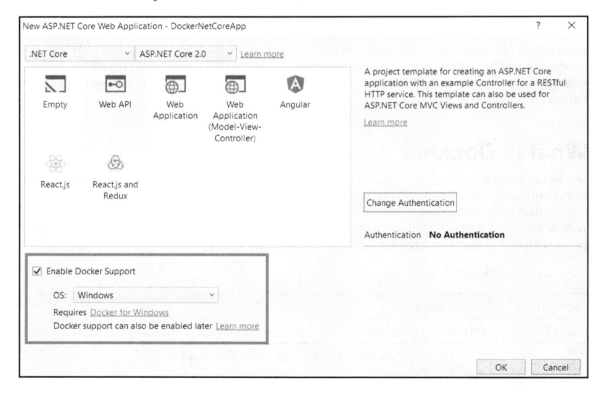

Alternatively, if the project is already created, we can add Docker support by right-clicking on the .NET Core project and clicking on the **Add | Docker Support** option.

Once we create or enable Docker support in our application, it creates the Docker files in our project and also adds another project, named docker-compose, as follows:

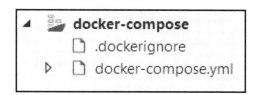

The docker-compose project contains set of YAML (.yml) files that contain the configuration related to the application hosted in the container and a reference to the path of the Dockerfile created for the project when Docker support was added. Here is the sample docker-compose.yml file that contains two services having details such as the image name, dockerfile path, and so on. This file is from the sample application we discussed previously:

```
version: '1'

services:
  vendor.api:
    image: vendor.api
    build:
      context: .
      dockerfile: srcmicroservicesVendorVendor.APIDockerfile

  identity.api:
    image: identity.api
    build:
      context: .
      dockerfile: srcmicroservicesAuthServerIdentity.AuthServerDockerfile
```

The following is the content of the Dockerfile residing inside the Vendor.API project we created in the sample application above:

```
FROM microsoft/aspnetcore:2.0-nanoserver-1709 AS base
WORKDIR /app
EXPOSE 80

FROM microsoft/aspnetcore-build:2.0-nanoserver-1709 AS build
WORKDIR /src
COPY *.sln ./
COPY src/microservices/Vendor/Vendor.API/Vendor.API.csproj
```

```
src/microservices/Vendor/Vendor.API/
RUN dotnet restore
COPY . .
WORKDIR /src/src/microservices/Vendor/Vendor.API
RUN dotnet build -c Release -o /app

FROM build AS publish
RUN dotnet publish -c Release -o /app

FROM base AS final
WORKDIR /app
COPY --from=publish /app .
ENTRYPOINT ["dotnet", "Vendor.API.dll"]
```

The preceding `Dockerfile` starts referencing a base image `microsoft/aspnetcore:2.0-nanoserver-1709` that will be used to create a Docker container. The `COPY` command is the actual path where the project files reside. It will then use dotnet CLI commands such as `dotnet restore` to restore all the NuGet packages inside the container, `dotnet build` to build the application, and `dotnet publish` to build and publishes the compiled output into a publish folder inside the container.

Running Docker images

We can run Docker images either from the command line or from Visual Studio directly. As we saw in the previous section, a new `docker-compose` project is created on adding Docker support into our project. Running the `docker-compose` project reads the `docker-compose` YAML file and hooks up containers for the services defined. Docker is a first-class citizen in Visual Studio. It not only supports running the Docker containers but fully-fledged debugging capabilities are also provided.

Alternatively, from the command line, we can run Docker containers by going to the root path where the `docker-compose.yml` file resides and running the following command:

```
docker-compose up
```

Once the containers are up, each application has its own IP assigned at runtime. To inspect the actual IP of each service running on a separate container, we can run the `docker inspect` command to retrieve it. However, the `docker inspect` command requires the container ID as a parameter. To get the list of the containers running, we can first call the `docker ps` command as follows:

```
docker ps
```

The preceding command displays the list of containers as shown in the following screenshot:

```
C:\Users\ovais>docker ps
CONTAINER ID        IMAGE              COMMAND              CREATED         STATUS          PORTS
                    NAMES
a12d3a37a644        vendor.api:dev     "C:\\remote_debugger\\…"  6 minutes ago   Up 5 minutes    0.0.0.0:40277
->80/tcp    dockercompose17175663515996174189_vendor.api_1
```

Finally, we can use the container ID and execute `docker inspect` command to get its IP address as follows:

```
docker inspect -f "{{range
.NetworkSettings.Networks}}{{.IPAddress}}{{end}}" containerid
```

The preceding command displays the IP address as follows:

```
C:\Users\ovais>docker inspect -f "{{range .NetworkSettings.Networks}}{{.IPAddress}}{{end}}" a12d3a37a644
192.168.44.35
```

Summary

In this chapter, we learned about the microservices architecture for developing highly performant and scalable applications for the cloud-based on microservices. We learned some of the fundamentals of microservices, their benefits, and patterns and practices used when designing the architecture. We discussed certain challenges in decomposing the enterprise applications into the microservices architecture style and learned patterns such as API composition and CQRS to address them. Later in the chapter, we developed a basic application in .NET Core and discussed the solution structure and components of microservices, and developed identity and vendor services.

In the next chapter, we will discuss securing and implementing resilience in .NET Core applications.

9
Monitoring Application Performance Using Tools

Monitoring application performance is a general process in big organizations to continuously monitor and improve the application experience for their customers. This is an important factor that revolves around different tools and techniques to measure the application performance and make decisions quickly.

In this chapter, we will learn some key indicators that are recommended to monitor the .NET Core application as well as explore App Metrics to get the real-time analytics and telemetry information about the key indicators.

In this chapter, we will look at the following topics:

- Key metrics to monitor application performance
- Tools and techniques to measure application performance, which includes:

    - Exploring App Metrics

    - Setting up App Metrics used with ASP.NET Core applications

    - Setting up Grafana and using the App Metrics dashboard

    - Setting up the InfluxDB database and integrating it with the ASP.NET Core application

    - Monitoring performance through the Grafana website

 To learn more about App Metrics or to contribute to the open source project, you can access the GitHub repository from the following link and see the complete documentation with some examples: https://github.com/AppMetrics/AppMetrics.

Application performance key metrics

The following are some key metrics to be considered for web-based applications.

Average response time

In every web application, response time is the key metric to be considered when monitoring application performance. Response time is the total time taken by the server to process the request. It is a time which is calculated when the request is received by the server which the time server then takes to process it and return a response. It can be affected by network latency, active users, the number of active requests, and CPU and memory usage on the server. The average response time is the total average time of all the requests being processed by the server at a particular time.

Apdex scores

Apdex is a user satisfaction score that can be categorized based on the performance of the application. The Apdex score can be categorized as satisfactory, tolerating, or frustrating.

Percentage of errors

This is the total percentage of the errors being reported in a particular amount of time. The user gets an overview of the total percentage of errors the user came across and can rectify them immediately.

Request rate

The request rate is a valuable metric used for scaling applications. If the request rate is high and the application's performance is not good, the application can be scaled out to support that number of requests. On the other hand, if the request rate is very low, that means there is an issue or that the number of active users are depleting and they are not using the application. In both cases, the decision can be taken abruptly to provide a consistent user experience.

Throughput/endpoints

Throughput is the number of requests the application can handle for a given amount of time. Usually, in commercial applications, the number of requests are pretty high and throughput allows you to benchmark the number of responses the application can handle without affecting the performance.

CPU and memory usage

CPU and memory usage is another important metric, which is used to analyse the peak hours where CPU or memory usage was high so that you can investigate the root cause.

Tools and techniques to measure performance

There are various tools available on the market that can be used to measure and monitor application performance. In this section, we will focus on App Metrics and analyse HTTP traffic, errors, and network performance.

Introducing App Metrics

App Metrics is an open source tool that can be plug in with the ASP.NET Core applications. It provides real-time insights about how the application is performing and provides a complete overview of the application's health status. It provides metrics in a JSON format and integrates with the Grafana dashboards for visual reporting. App Metrics is based on .NET Standard and runs cross-platform. It provides various extensions and reporting dashboards that can run on Windows and Linux operating system as well.

Setting up App Metrics with ASP.NET Core

We can set up App Metrics in the ASP.NET Core application in three easy steps, which are as follows:

1. Install App Metrics.

   App Metrics can be installed as NuGet packages. Here are the two packages that can be added through NuGet in your .NET Core project:

   ```
   Install-Package App.Metrics
   Install-Pacakge App.Metrics.AspnetCore.Mvc
   ```

2. Add App Metrics in `Program.cs`.

   Add `UseMetrics` to `Program.cs` in the `BuildWebHost` method, as follows:

   ```
   public static IWebHost BuildWebHost(string[] args) =>
     WebHost.CreateDefaultBuilder(args)
       .UseMetrics()
       .UseStartup<Startup>()
       .Build();
   ```

3. Add App Metrics in `Startup.cs`.

   Finally, we can add a metrics resource filter in the `ConfigureServices` method of the `Startup` class as follows:

   ```
   public void ConfigureServices(IServiceCollection services)
   {
     services.AddMvc(options => options.AddMetricsResourceFilter());
   }
   ```

4. Run your application.

Build and run the application. We can test whether App Metrics is running well by using URLs, as shown in the following table. Just append the URL to the application's root URL:

URL	Description
/metrics	Shows metrics using the configured metrics formatter
/metrics-text	Shows metrics using the configured text formatter
/env	Shows environment information, which includes the operating system, machine name, assembly name, and version

Appending /metrics or /metrics-text to the application's root URL gives complete information about application metrics. /metrics returns the JSON response that can be parsed and represented in a view with some custom parsing.

Tracking middleware

With App Metrics, we can manually define the typical web metrics which are essential to record telemetry information. However, for ASP.NET Core, there is a tracking middleware that can be used and configured in the project, which contains some built-in key metrics which are specific to the web application.

Metrics that are recorded by the Tracking middleware are as follows:

- **Apdex**: This is used to monitor the user's satisfaction based on the overall performance of the application. Apdex is an open industry standard that measures the user's satisfaction based on the application's response time.

We can configure the threshold of time, *T*, for each request cycle, and the metrics are calculated based on following conditions:

User Satisfaction	Description
Satisfactory	If the response time is less than or equal to the threshold time (T)
Tolerating	If the response time is between the threshold time (T) and 4 times that of the threshold time (T) in seconds
Frustrating	If the respo nse time is greater than 4 times that of the threshold time (T)

- **Response times:** This provides the overall throughput of the request being processed by the application and the duration it takes per route within the application.

- **Active requests:** This provides the list of active requests which have been received on the server in a particular amount of time.

- **Errors:** This provides the aggregated results of errors in a percentage that includes the overall error request rate, the overall count of each uncaught exception type, the total number of error requests per HTTP status code, and so on.

- **POST and PUT sizes:** This provides the request sizes for HTTP POST and PUT requests.

Adding tracking middleware

We can add tracking middleware as a NuGet package as follows:

```
Install-Package App.Metrics.AspNetCore.Tracking
```

Tracking middleware provides a set of middleware that is added to record telemetry for the specific metric. We can add the following middleware in the `Configure` method to measure performance metrics:

```
app.UseMetricsApdexTrackingMiddleware();
app.UseMetricsRequestTrackingMiddleware();
app.UseMetricsErrorTrackingMiddleware();
app.UseMetricsActiveRequestMiddleware();
app.UseMetricsPostAndPutSizeTrackingMiddleware();
app.UseMetricsOAuth2TrackingMiddleware();
```

Alternatively, we can also use meta-pack middleware, which adds all the available tracking middleware so that we have information about all the different metrics which are in the preceding code:

```
app.UseMetricsAllMiddleware();
```

Next, we will add tracking middleware in our `ConfigureServices` method as follows:

```
services.AddMetricsTrackingMiddleware();
```

In the main `Program.cs` class, we will modify the `BuildWebHost` method and add the `UseMetricsWebTracking` method as follows:

```
public static IWebHost BuildWebHost(string[] args) =>
  WebHost.CreateDefaultBuilder(args)
    .UseMetrics()
    .UseMetricsWebTracking()
    .UseStartup<Startup>()
    .Build();
```

Setting up configuration

Once the middleware is added, we need to set up the default threshold and other configuration values so that reporting can be generated accordingly. The web tracking properties can be configured in the `appsettings.json` file. Here is the content of the `appsettings.json` file that contains the `MetricWebTrackingOptions` JSON key:

```
"MetricsWebTrackingOptions": {
  "ApdexTrackingEnabled": true,
  "ApdexTSeconds": 0.1,
  "IgnoredHttpStatusCodes": [ 404 ],
  "IgnoredRoutesRegexPatterns": [],
  "OAuth2TrackingEnabled": true
    },
```

`ApdexTrackingEnabled` is set to true so that the customer satisfaction report will be generated, and `ApdexTSeconds` is the threshold that decides whether the request response time was satisfactory, tolerating, or frustrating. `IgnoredHttpStatusCodes` contains the list of status codes that will be ignored if the response returns a `404` status. `IgnoredRoutesRegexPatterns` are used to ignore specific URIs that match the regular expression, and `OAuth2TrackingEnabled` can be set to monitor and record the metrics for each client and provide information specific to the request rate, error rate, and POST and PUT sizes for each client.

Run the application and do some navigation. Appending /metrics-text in your application URL will display the complete report in textual format. Here is the sample snapshot of what textual metrics looks like:

```
←  →  C  ⓘ localhost:60676/metrics-text

# TIMESTAMP: 636576372311231394
# MEASUREMENT: [Application.HttpRequests] Apdex
# TAGS:
                server = OVAISPC
                   app = SampleWebApp
                   env = development
                 mtype = apdex
                  unit = result
# FIELDS:
               samples = 0
                 score = 1
             satisfied = 0
            tolerating = 0
           frustrating = 0
-------------------------------------------------------------
# TIMESTAMP: 636576372311231394
# MEASUREMENT: [Application.HttpRequests] One Minute Error Percentage Rate
# TAGS:
                server = OVAISPC
                   app = SampleWebApp
                   env = development
                 mtype = gauge
                  unit = req
# FIELDS:
                 value = 100
-------------------------------------------------------------
# TIMESTAMP: 636576372311231394
# MEASUREMENT: [Application.HttpRequests] Active
# TAGS:
                server = OVAISPC
                   app = SampleWebApp
                   env = development
                 mtype = counter
                  unit = Active Requests
# FIELDS:
                 value = 0
-------------------------------------------------------------
# TIMESTAMP: 636576372311231394
# MEASUREMENT: [Application.HttpRequests] Errors
# TAGS:
      http_status_code = 304
                server = OVAISPC
                   app = SampleWebApp
                   env = development
                 mtype = counter
                  unit = err
```

Adding visual reports

There are various extensions and reporting plugins available that provide a visual reporting dashboard. Some of them are *GrafanaCloud Hosted Metrics, InfluxDB, Prometheus, ElasticSearch, Graphite, HTTP, Console,* and *Text File.* In this chapter, we will configure the *InfluxDB* extension and see how visual reporting can be achieved.

Setting up InfluxDB

InfluxDB is the open source time series database developed by Influx Data. It is written in the *Go* language and is widely used to store time series data for real-time analytics. Grafana is the server that provides reporting dashboards that can be viewed through a browser. InfluxDB can easily be imported as an extension in Grafana to display visual reporting from the InfluxDB database.

Setting up the Windows subsystem for Linux

In this section, we will set up InfluxDB on the Windows subsystem for the Linux operating system.

1. First of all, we need to enable the Windows subsystem for Linux by executing the following command from the PowerShell as an Administrator:

```
Enable-WindowsOptionalFeature -Online -FeatureName
Microsoft-Windows-Subsystem-Linux
```

After running the preceding command, restart your computer.

2. Next, we will install Linux distro from the Microsoft store. In our case, we will install Ubuntu from the Microsoft Store. Go to the Microsoft Store, search for Ubuntu, and install it.

3. Once the installation is done, click on **Launch**:

4. This will open up the console window, which will ask you to create a user account for Linux OS (Operating System).
5. Specify the username and password that will be used.
6. Run the following command to update Ubuntu to the latest stable version from the bash shell. To run bash, open the command prompt, write `bash`, and hit *Enter*:

7. Finally, it will ask you to create an Ubuntu username and password. Specify the username and password and hit enter.

Installing InfluxDB

Here, we will go through some steps to install the InfluxDB database in Ubuntu:

1. To set up InfluxDB, open a command prompt in Administrator mode and run the bash shell.

2. Execute the following commands to the InfluxDB data store on your local PC:

```
$ curl -sL https://repos.influxdata.com/influxdb.key | sudo apt-key
add -
$ source /etc/lsb-release
$ echo "deb https://repos.influxdata.com/${DISTRIB_ID,,}
$ {DISTRIB_CODENAME} stable" | sudo tee
/etc/apt/sources.list.d/influxdb.list
```

3. Install InfluxDB by executing the following command:

```
$ sudo apt-get update && sudo apt-get install influxdb
```

4. Execute the following command to run InfluxDB:

```
$ sudo influxd
```

5. Start the InfluxDB shell by running the following command:

```
$ sudo influx
```

It will open up the shell where database-specific commands can be executed.

6. Create a database by executing the following command. Specify a meaningful name for the database. In our case, it is `appmetricsdb`:

```
> create database appmetricsdb
```

Installing Grafana

Grafana is an open source tool used to display dashboards in a web interface. There are various dashboards available that can be imported from the Grafana website to display real-time analytics. Grafana can simply be downloaded as a zip file from `http://docs.grafana.org/installation/windows/`. Once it is downloaded, we can start the Grafana server by clicking on the `grafana-server.exe` executable from the `bin` directory.

Grafana provides a website that listens on port *3000*. If the Grafana server is running, we can access the site by navigating to `http://localhost:3000`.

Adding the InfluxDB dashboard

There is an out-of-the-box InfluxDB dashboard available in Grafana which can be imported from the following link: `https://grafana.com/dashboards/2125`.

Copy the dashboard ID and use this to import it into the Grafana website.

We can import the InfluxDB dashboard by going to the **Manage** option on the Grafana website, as follows:

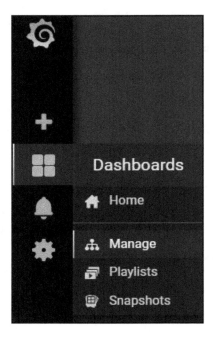

From the **Manage** option, click on the **+ Dashboard** button and hit the **New Dashboard** option. Clicking on **Import Dashboard** will lead to Grafana asking you for the dashboard ID:

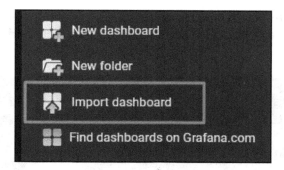

Paste the dashboard ID (for example, `2125`) copied earlier into the box and hit *Tab*. The system will show the dashboard's details, and clicking on the **Import** button will import it into the system:

Configuring InfluxDB

We will now configure the InfluxDB dashboard and add a data source that connects to the database that we just created.

To proceed, we will go to the **Data Sources** section on the Grafana website and click on the **Add New Datasource** option. Here is the configuration that adds the data source for the InfluxDB database:

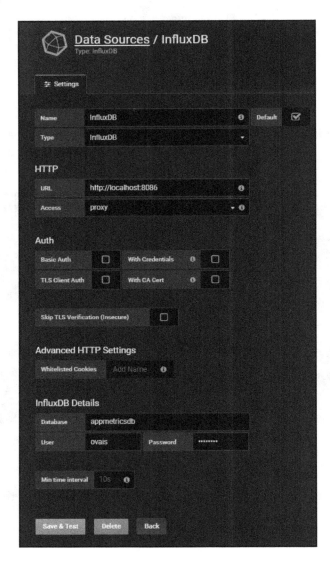

Modifying the Configure and ConfigureServices methods in Startup

Up to now, we have set up Ubuntu and the InfluxDB database on our machine. We also set up the InfluxDB data source and added a dashboard through the Grafana website. Next, we will configure our ASP.NET Core web application to push real-time information to the InfluxDB database.

Here is the modified `ConfigureServices` method that initializes the `MetricsBuilder` to define the attribute related to the application name, environment, and connection details:

```
public void ConfigureServices(IServiceCollection services)
{
  var metrics = new MetricsBuilder()
  .Configuration.Configure(
  options =>
  {
    options.WithGlobalTags((globalTags, info) =>
    {
      globalTags.Add("app", info.EntryAssemblyName);
      globalTags.Add("env", "stage");
    });
  })
  .Report.ToInfluxDb(
  options =>
  {
    options.InfluxDb.BaseUri = new Uri("http://127.0.0.1:8086");
    options.InfluxDb.Database = "appmetricsdb";
    options.HttpPolicy.Timeout = TimeSpan.FromSeconds(10);
  })
  .Build();
  services.AddMetrics(metrics);
  services.AddMetricsReportScheduler();
  services.AddMetricsTrackingMiddleware();
  services.AddMvc(options => options.AddMetricsResourceFilter());
}
```

In the preceding code, we have set the application name app as the assembly name, and the environment env as the stage. http://127.0.0.1:8086 is the URL of the InfluxDB server that listens for the telemetry being pushed by the application. appmetricsdb is the database that we created in the preceding section. Then, we added the AddMetrics middleware and specified the metrics containing the configuration. AddMetricsTrackingMiddleware is used to track the web telemetry information which is displayed on the dashboard, and AddMetricsReportScheduled is used to push the telemetry information to the database.

Here is the Configure method that contains UseMetricsAllMiddleware to use App Metrics. UseMetricsAllMiddleware adds all the middleware available in App Metrics:

```
public void Configure(IApplicationBuilder app, IHostingEnvironment env)
{
  if (env.IsDevelopment())
  {
    app.UseBrowserLink();
    app.UseDeveloperExceptionPage();
  }
  else
  {
    app.UseExceptionHandler("/Error");
  }
  app.UseStaticFiles();
  app.UseMetricsAllMiddleware();
  app.UseMvc();
}
```

Rather than calling UseAllMetricsMiddleware, we can also add individual middleware explicitly based on the requirements. Here is the list of middleware that can be added:

```
app.UseMetricsApdexTrackingMiddleware();
app.UseMetricsRequestTrackingMiddleware();
app.UseMetricsErrorTrackingMiddleware();
app.UseMetricsActiveRequestMiddleware();
app.UseMetricsPostAndPutSizeTrackingMiddleware();
app.UseMetricsOAuth2TrackingMiddleware();
```

Testing the ASP.NET Core App and reporting on the Grafana dashboard

To test the ASP.NET Core application and to see visual reporting on the Grafana dashboard, we will go through following steps:

1. Start the Grafana server by going to `{installation_directory}\bin\grafana-server.exe`.
2. Start bash from the command prompt and run the `sudo influx` command.
3. Start another bash from the command prompt and run the `sudo influx` command.
4. Run the ASP.NET Core application.
5. Access `http://localhost:3000` and click on the App Metrics dashboard.
6. This will start gathering telemetry information and will display the performance metrics, as shown in the following screenshots:

   The following graph shows the total throughput in **Request Per Minute (RPM)**, error percentage, and active requests:

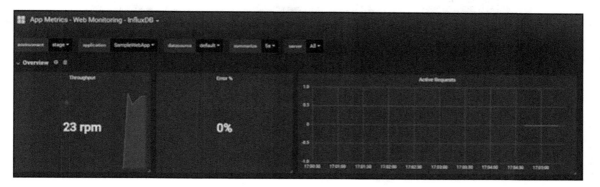

Here is the Apdex score colorizing the user satisfaction into three different colors, where red is frustrating, orange is tolerating, and green is satisfactory. The following graph shows the blue line being drawn on the green bar, which means that the application performance is satisfactory:

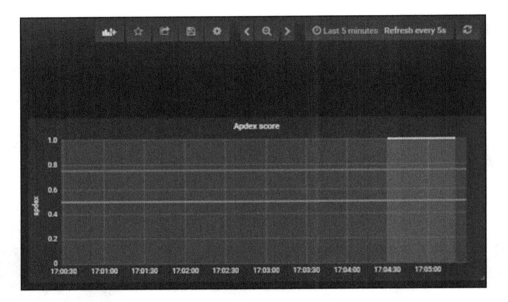

The following snapshot shows the throughput graph for all the requests being made, and each request has been colorized with the different colors: red, orange, and green. In this case, there are two HTTP GET requests for the about and contact us pages:

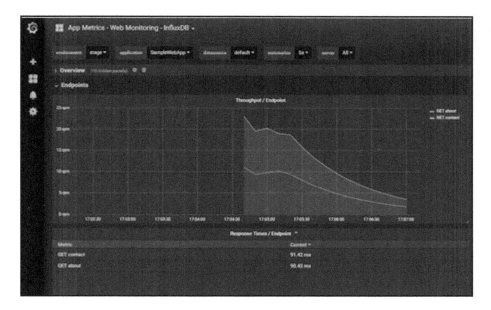

Here is the response time graph showing the response time of both requests:

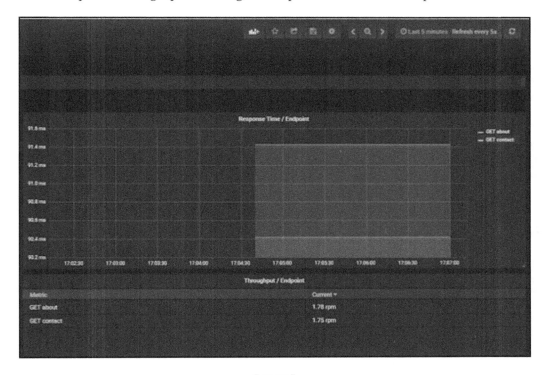

Summary

In this chapter, we have learned some key metrics which are essential for monitoring application performance. We explored and set up App Metrics, which is a free tool that runs cross-platform and provides a lot of extensions that can be added to achieve more reporting. We went through the step-by-step guide on how to configure and set up App Metrics and related components like InfluxDb and Grafana to store and view telemetry in the Grafana web-based tool and integrate it with ASP.NET Core application.

Other Books You May Enjoy

If you enjoyed this book, you may be interested in these other books by Packt:

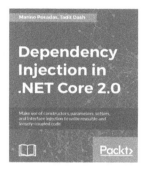

Dependency Injection in .NET Core 2.0
Marino Posadas, Tadit Dash

ISBN: 978-1-78712-130-0

- Understand the concept of DI and its implications in modern software construction
- Learn how DI is already implemented in today's frameworks.
- Analyze how DI can be used with current software to improve maintainability and scalability.
- Learn the use of DI in .NET Core
- Get used to the possibilities that DI offers the ASP.NET Core developer in different scenarios.
- Learn about good practices and refactoring legacy code.

Mastering ASP.NET Core 2.0
Ricardo Peres

ISBN: 978-1-78728-368-8

- Get to know the new features of ASP.NET Core 2.0
- Find out how to configure ASP.NET Core
- Configure routes to access ASP.NET Core resources
- Create controllers and action methods and see how to maintain the state
- Create views to display contents
- Implement and validate forms and retrieve information from them
- Write reusable modules for ASP.NET Core
- Deploy ASP.NET Core to other environments

Leave a review - let other readers know what you think

Please share your thoughts on this book with others by leaving a review on the site that you bought it from. If you purchased the book from Amazon, please leave us an honest review on this book's Amazon page. This is vital so that other potential readers can see and use your unbiased opinion to make purchasing decisions, we can understand what our customers think about our products, and our authors can see your feedback on the title that they have worked with Packt to create. It will only take a few minutes of your time, but is valuable to other potential customers, our authors, and Packt. Thank you!

Index

www.ingramcontent.com/pod-product-compliance
Lightning Source LLC
Chambersburg PA
CBHW080627060326
40690CB00021B/4847